ADVANCED NEGOTIATION AND MEDIATION THEORY AND PRACTICE
A REALISTIC INTEGRATED APPROACH

NITA

ADVANCED NEGOTIATION AND MEDIATION THEORY AND PRACTICE
A REALISTIC INTEGRATED APPROACH

THOMAS F. GUERNSEY
PRESIDENT, DEAN, AND PROFESSOR OF LAW
ALBANY UNIVERSITY SCHOOL OF LAW

PAUL J. ZWIER
PROFESSOR OF LAW, EMORY UNIVERSITY SCHOOL OF LAW
DIRECTOR OF EDUCATION, NITA

NATIONAL INSTITUTE FOR TRIAL ADVOCACY

NITA Editorial Board

Reproduction Permission
National Institute for Trial Advocacy
(800) 225-6482
Web site: www.nita.org

Guernsey, Thomas F. and Paul J. Zwier, *Advanced Negotiation and Mediation Theory and Practice: A Realistic Integrated Approach* (NITA 2005).

ISBN 978-1-55681-950-6

9/05   10/08

Library of Congress Cataloging-in-Publication Data
Guernsey, Thomas F.
        Advanced negotiation and mediation theory and practice: a realistic integrated approach / Thomas F. Guernsey, Paul J. Zwier
        p. cm.
        Includes index.
        ISBN 1-55681-950-1 (alk. paper)
        1. Dispute resolution (Law). 2. Negotiation. 3. Mediation. I. Zwier, Paul J., 1954- II. Title.
K2390.G84 2005
347'.09--dc22

Advanced Negotiation and Mediation Theory and Practice

CONTENTS

To Ruth and Lori Guernsey and Sue Gordon

To Marlene, Kara, John, and Erin

PREFACE

Whether handling the purchase of property for a major real estate development, trying to reach agreement in a bank merger, putting together a joint venture, negotiating with opposing counsel in a medical malpractice case, dealing with a disgruntled office employee, or negotiating one's own partnership agreement with a colleague, lawyers spend much of their time negotiating.

Viewed broadly, negotiation is the process by which two or more parties solve a particular problem involving competing interests, needs, or desires. Negotiation obviously takes place within a wide variety of relationships and under a wide variety of circumstances. Throughout all negotiations, however, there remains a common thread. In each circumstance, people come together with potentially different goals and attempt to solve a specific problem. The tone may be quite different when negotiating on behalf of a client in a lawsuit than when negotiating for purchasing a car. The process, as we shall see, however, is essentially the same.

This book proceeds on the premise that negotiation ought to be a process in which you make conscious, thoughtful choices. Too often, however, it is a disorganized series of reactions to what someone else, usually opposing counsel, has done. In order to make rational choices, you should look at a particular negotiation as a whole; get a sense of the wide range of choices you need to make, when you need to make them, and how your choices at one stage affect other stages. Just as importantly, you should know when to choose alternatives to what is normally done.

In other words, today's lawyers need to be able to think strategically, whether they are transactional lawyers or litigators. Not only must they understand how to put a case together for trial, or deal together for closing, but they also need to understand the clients' business and long term goals in order to be able to give their clients wise advice. They need to be able to determine where the client wants to go and how best to get there. They need to be able to get information (both facts and feelings) from the client as well to give clear, precise, comprehensive advice to the client. To that end, lawyers need to be skilled interviewers, brainstormers, fact investigation planners, and comprehensive thinkers, as well as informed, strategic thinkers, and wise counselors, before they can be negotiators. It is vital to their success as a negotiator to accurately determine where the clients want to go—the ends they desire—and then reverse engineer from the end goals to best get the clients to those ends.

As a result, we have placed special emphasis in this book on counseling. The lawyer needs to identify the client's (or other relevant parties') goals and underlying objectives, assign priorities or weights to those objectives, and specify the criteria in terms of which solution will be evaluated. For the counseling to be effective for the client, the lawyer needs to be able to generate alternative solutions or courses of action and then assess the alternatives. The lawyer needs to help the client evaluate the consequences of each alternative according to how well they satisfy the client's underlying objectives. As a part of this counseling process the lawyer must gather information necessary to assess each alternative to help the client select the optimal course of action according to the expected effectiveness in meeting underlying goals.

We have also placed special emphasis on mediation. After all, the lawyer needs to implement the client's decision. While the lawyers can often do this by themselves, either through the deal making process, or through negotiation short of trial, frequently part of the implementation is for the lawyer to select the right dispute resolution process, including arbitration, or, as is more often the case today, with the help of a mediator.

The lawyer needs to be able to think strategically about each part of the contracting or dispute resolution process, to best implement the client's decision and monitor its implementation, being prepared to reengage in the decision making process as unforeseen problems are encountered.

This book focuses on a number of parts of the negotiation and dispute resolution process. It describes in the first four chapters a strategic planning and integrated systematic approach to negotiation. The same approach should apply regardless of the relationship between the parties and regardless of the subject matter of the negotiation. This book describes an approach to negotiation that asks you, as the lawyer, to step back from the negotiation process and determine, "What stages do I normally go through in a negotiation?" By analyzing the stages through which a negotiation typically goes proceeds, you can study and practice those stages, thus improving your skills in the area. In other words, this book provides a framework within which to view negotiation. This approach also allows you to plan and implement effective negotiating techniques.

Integral to this planning process are the client's views of the case. This book focuses on the skills involved in engaging the client in the decision making process. It shows how understanding negotiation theory and practice can help the lawyer teach the client how to make better strategic use of negotiation. It breaks down the counseling process into stages and shows what information the client needs in order to make an informed decision.

The approach we use to step back, plan, and to teach the client, also serves as an organizational tool allowing you to simplify a complex process sufficiently to view it as a whole. Just as there is no one way to examine a witness in court, there is no one correct way to negotiate a particular transaction or dispute. An approach for the "typical" examination in trial practice, however, is helpful as an organizing tool. In examining a witness, a useful approach is to (1) introduce the witness (accredit), (2) set the scene, (3) develop the facts either chronologically or topically, (4) anticipate any negative testimony, and (5) end on a high point for your client. This simple approach provides a way to structure an examination, which is not rigid, and which must yield to the realities of a particular case.

The approach suggested here serves the same function. We will, for example, identify "ice breaking" as an important stage in the negotiation process. A series of choices occur during this stage, based on the need to develop the appropriate relationship with the person with whom you are negotiating. It would be foolish to suggest that the only time you worry about this relationship issue is at the beginning of a face-to-face exchange. The approach suggests you should do it then, but it also suggests that you should be looking for other opportunities to accomplish the goals of this particular stage.

Chapters 5 through 8 describe four stages of negotiation: Icebreaking and Setting the Agenda, Information Bargaining, Exchange, and Crisis and Outcome.

Chapter 9 focuses on the planning and strategic decision making process involved when negotiating in an international setting.

Chapter 10 places special emphasis on planning for and making choices about multiparty negotiations. More and more clients are involved in multiple party deals and multiple party disputes. The dynamics of negotiation in multiparty contexts change the strategic planning that needs to occur. This chapter describes these strategic planning issues and how they may affect the choices the client and lawyer may make in implementing the client's objectives.

Chapter 11 considers using a mediator to implement the client's goals. It first focuses on thinking strategically about when to bring a mediator into the process. It then looks at how best to work with the mediator before and during mediation, to implement the client's goals and objectives.

Finally, in Chapter 12, we focus on changes in the rules of Professional Responsibility, and on how these affect the ethical issues in today's negotiations.

CHAPTER 1
NEGOTIATING STRATEGIES AND STYLES

Many authors have attempted to describe negotiation in one all-inclusive theory. For example, academics in the forties, fifties, and sixties began using game theory and other mathematical models to describe behavior during a negotiation. More recent approaches include an economic theory of negotiation and social-psychological theories of negotiation. President Jimmy Carter urged lawyers in the eighties that they could learn much from international negotiators. Other theories on negotiation include attempts to determine whether race, gender, and culture affect the negotiation process and dispute resolution outcomes. These varied theories each suggest different strategies to take in the negotiation.

> **Interdisciplinary Approaches to Studying Negotiation**
>
> —Game Theory
>
> —Economic Theory
>
> —International Politics
>
> —Ethnic Differences
>
> —Gender Differences
>
> —Social Psychology

While a full discussion of these theories is beyond the scope of this book, you should realize that on a practical level these theories suggest that there are two general approaches (and combinations of these approaches) that are used in negotiation. The game and economic theories view negotiation as an adversarial, position bargaining, zero-sum process. As its name indicates, the problem-solving theory incorporates the learning from international conflict resolution and other conflict resolution structures. It views negotiation as a problem-solving or interest-based "win-win" process. This book's approach to negotiation combines these two theories, suggesting that while an adversarial strategy is appropriate in some circumstances, a problem-solving strategy may be appropriate in others. Moreover, understanding the different strategies involved in negotiation can lead to better client counseling. In addition, it will help the client choose what kind of mediation the client might engage in, and how to think strategically about the mediation process.

A. Adversarial Negotiation—An Economic Theory and Strategy of Negotiation

Under the economic theory, you can picture every negotiation as involving one or more fungible or interchangeable items, such as money, and the negotiation can be represented in graphic terms. The item being negotiated, damages, for example, is placed on a continuum. The negotiators take positions along the continuum until their positions meet: adversarial bargaining is also referred to as position bargaining. If we take, for example, negotiating over the settlement of a medical malpractice action, the continuum starts with the physician's insurer paying nothing and moves to an infinite number of dollars. The plaintiff and defendant each make a decision about where they will begin negotiating along this continuum—their opening offer (OO). They each will choose places along that continuum where they will move to (their commitment point (CP) and/or target point (TP)) and a place beyond which they will not go—their bottom line (BL).

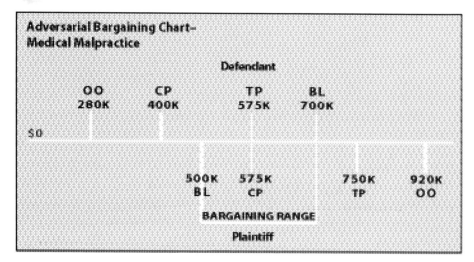

The area between each side's opening point and bottom line is referred to as their "bargaining range." In the malpractice example, a settlement range exists where the plaintiff's bargaining range overlaps with the defendant's bargaining range. By definition, any settlement that occurs will be within this settlement range. Under this scenario, any settlement will be between $500,000 and $700,000.

Look how this framework is based on economics and applies equally well to deals. It attempts to look at ways of placing economic value on a combination of tangible and intangible items. Think about the deal reached between an employer and employee. The same charting lays out the positions of the parties and helps them make choices in arriving at their deal.

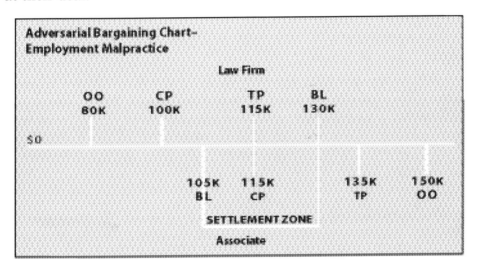

Viewing negotiation in this manner has several practical advantages and suggests certain basic elements of the negotiating process. First, this graphic approach suggests that early in any negotiation you must determine your own bottom line. Second, the graph suggests that you spend much of your time in a negotiation trying to determine the other side's bottom line. While this may seem obvious, what is not obvious, and what the graph suggests, is that your bottom line is the result of rational decision making. Likewise, if your bottom line is rationally based, then a working assumption should be that your opponent's bottom line is also rationally based. If this is the case, you should spend much of the negotiation seeking information that will allow you to recreate the other side's decision-making perspective and, hopefully, their bottom line. As we will discuss later, not only does this inform your counseling session with the client, but when seeking information from the other side you should seek economic, psychological, and social relationship information about the opponent and his or her client that led to a particular bottom line.

This zero-sum or adversarial approach, however, has obvious disadvantages. It suggests negotiation is a contest in which participants stake out positions and then go through a process of concession and compromise. This adversarial model also suggests that there is a winner and a loser. For example, if one side gains a dollar, the other side loses a dollar.

This adversarial approach may well be contrary to the goodwill you are trying to maintain or develop in a particular negotiation. For example, if you are negotiating a peaceful merger of two hospitals, such an adversarial approach may doom the negotiations before they even begin.

This approach also does not consider the fluid nature of negotiation. For example, it assumes that a negotiator determines a bottom line early in the negotiation and sticks to it. In reality, of course, the negotiator's view of an acceptable solution to the negotiation may change as he or she gets more information from the other parties to the negotiation.

B. Problem-Solving Negotiation as a Strategy

A second theory views negotiation from a problem-solving perspective. Under this theory, the negotiators are engaged in joint problem-solving. Problem-solvers, just as adversarials, are certainly interested in their own needs, interests, and desires. True problem-solvers, however, are just as interested in the other party's needs, interests, and desires. Problem-solvers can be thought of as bargaining about *interests* rather than *positions*. As such, problem-solvers eschew positions and seek to have the parties openly express their needs, interests, and desires so that the parties may jointly create an appropriate solution to the issue being negotiated. Problem-solvers see the "position" of the adversarial negotiator as only one of many solutions to the underlying problem.

Three examples help make the point. Imagine that two parties are sent to a late night grocer shortly before closing. Both want an orange.

They each reach for the orange at the same time and each establishes a firm grip on the orange. How do they resolve who gets the orange? Their option seems to be to resort to violence. The stronger or the more ruthless will be the only one getting the orange.

Now imagine, instead that the parties talk to each other. One wants the orange for its juice, to make a cake. One wants the orange for the rind, to make a garnish for a drink. If they are able to find out why each wants the orange, the problem-solver will be able to suggest a win/win solution to the problem. They split paying for the orange, and one peels it and each takes the part they need.

Remember the Orange

—Positions versus Underlying Needs

—International Problem Solving

—Building Trust During the Process

Here lies the key, according to those attempting to solve the problem of Middle East peace. The Israelis say, we get Jerusalem. The Palestinians say, we get it. The only resolution seems to be to resort to violence. If however, the parties could get past their positions, if they could describe why they want to live in Jerusalem: to worship in their holy sites, to raise their children in safety and security, to learn their traditions and sacred beliefs, to grow into all that God/Allah intended them to be, then the goals and underlying needs that each side has may be met with win/win solutions.

A primary advantage to problem-solving is that by addressing the underlying needs of the parties (i.e., the reason or interest behind the position) other, perhaps more creative, solutions can be developed. Lawyers have used creative problem-solving in a number of contexts, to the point where the approach has become institutionalized within a segment of the profession.

A third such example is in medical malpractice actions. For years, plaintiff's lawyers would demand a set amount of money, such as one million dollars. Defense counsel would offer, if anything, a lower amount. The parties would then move toward some middle ground by a series of concessions and compromises. This was classic adversarial negotiation.

Lawyers, however, have begun using problem-solving approaches, asking, for example, what underlies the plaintiff's need to have one million dollars? If they could identify those needs and solve them, it might cost less money. For example, if the plaintiff claims he needs the money to insure long-term medical treatment, to educate his children, and to compensate for lost wages and the like, the insurer can structure a payment schedule that guarantees these things. The ultimate cost under this structure may be far less than the plaintiff's adversarial demand and can afford a variety of payment methods other than a single lump-sum payment. Hence, structured settlements have become more popular.

There are numerous other examples of common uses of problem-solving strategies. Some joint child custody arrangements are essentially problem-solving solutions. Rather than a negotiation premised on dividing time between parents, many parties are asking how to create a living arrangement that accommodates all parties' legitimate needs.

The power of creative problem-solving is particularly evident in situations where adversarial negotiation might lead to deadlock. Remember that for adversarial negotiators to agree, their bargaining ranges must overlap. If the ranges do not overlap, adversarial negotiators will not reach settlement. Take a non-legal example. In the late 1970s, mortgage interest rates were in the upper teens. The banking industry's negotiation with the borrowing public had been basically adversarial, and business suffered. In that negotiation with the public, the industry staked out a bottom line position of 17–18 percent on home mortgages. The public's bottom line, however, was somewhere near 12 percent. The bargaining ranges did not overlap.

son needs to sell this car to earn a bonus or increase a monthly commission, whether the dealer is getting any factory incentives, or any other information that you could use to help decide if the dealer would take a lower price.

While in situations of trust, where parties perceive the need to develop a long-term relationship, and empathetic understanding will greatly redound to the benefit of the parties, problem-solving techniques will operate effectively and efficiently. However, where parties are in short term relationships, or perceive it to their advantage to block and conceal to gain a transactional advantage, then position-bargaining techniques are safer, even if there is a greater risk of deadlock. At the heart of the matter is a view of human nature. Will bargainers be able to set aside selfish concerns and bargain more altruistically, for the long-term good of their opponent? Or will bargainers only fake these more altruistic concerns in order to position themselves to take advantage of the other?

Our approach is to take a realistic integrative approach: to see bargaining in stages. We will take the approach that position bargaining and problem-solving are not mutually exclusive. At the heart of the matter is information exchange. Position bargaining can lead to information that will test the good faith of the opposition. If the parties develop trust in each other, they can quickly move to problem-solving strategies. If not, bargainers can yet move to problem-solving if position bargaining fails. In these situations of deadlock the parties can try to bridge the deadlock with active listening, restatement, and reflection techniques that may yet lead to more win-win solutions. Integrative bargaining can build bridges to creative solutions with skills and techniques for problem-solving and monitoring, or then further test the positions the opposition has taken with position-bargaining techniques.

C. Styles of Negotiation

Besides the two general approaches to negotiation we have referred to as strategy, researchers have identified two styles that are commonly seen in negotiation: competitive and cooperative.[1] Competitive negotiators are aggressive and assertive, and the pitch, pace, tone, and volume of their voices will reflect that style. Cooperative negotiators have a correspondingly different approach. Cooperative negotiators, as

---

1   G. Williams, EFFECTIVE NEGOTIATION AND SETTLEMENT (1981).

the term reflects, are cooperative in approach, and the pitch, pace, tone, and volume of their voices will be controlled accordingly.

Recognizing that there are two extremes of both strategies and styles begins to suggest the range of possible combinations that you can take in a negotiation. Competitive adversarials tend to be rigid and demanding. Cooperative adversarials tend to view the negotiation process as a series of concessions and compromise. Competitive problem-solvers tend to be careful and engage in limited problem-solving, often hesitant to reveal too much information because of lack of trust. Cooperative problem-solvers tend to be open and trusting.

Statistically, nothing indicates that one type of negotiator is more likely to be successful than any other. As discussed earlier, however, there are specific advantages to each. A particular negotiator may be naturally more cooperative, albeit adversarial, with an opposing counsel he or she works with regularly, while being a competitive adversarial with the lawyer he or she meets for the first time.

Many people intuitively move from one combination of style and strategy to another. For example, you may have experienced a frustrating negotiation apparently not going anywhere when someone finally said something like "[EXPLETIVE DELETED] I can't stand this! What is it you really want out of this deal?" That person has moved from being a cooperative adversarial to a competitive adversarial to a competitive problem-solver. In fact, some would argue that the natural place to switch to problem-solving strategy is where adversarial bargaining has only produced deadlock. In these situations it is important for the bargainer to remember our early example of the orange. Switching the language to one of goals and objectives may save the bargainers despite apparent deadlock.

Combining Style and Strategy:
Adversarial and Problem Solving
Competitive and Cooperative

	Adversarial Strategy	Problem Solving Strategy
Competitive Style	Rigid and Risky	Limited Needs and Solutions
Cooperative Style	Concession and Compromise	All Needs and Solutions

---

One way to see these strategies and styles is to see them in combinations with various strengths and weaknesses.

D. Blending Strategies and Styles

This book takes the approach that both the adversarial strategy and the problem-solving strategy have distinct advantages, and, as with all aspects of negotiation, a choice should be made whether a particular negotiation should proceed from an adversarial perspective or a problem-solving perspective. The following examples suggest how bargainers might combine styles and strategies to reach various results.

The Caring and Compassionate Grandmother. You are five years old. You go to visit your grandmother. You attempt to negotiate a second cookie, and then later, a later bedtime. How might your Grandmother choose the best style and strategy? She might be very cooperative in style. "Oh honey, come here and give Grandma a hug and kiss. But no, you have already had enough cookies. It is time for bed. Lights out." Grandma has chosen a position-bargaining strategy with a cooperative style. It is firm. It tolerates no discussion of reasons or underlying needs.

The Family's Used Car Negotiator. You are called on to shop for cars for your family members. Before you go, you put on a black T-shirt with white lettering that says, "That's Mr. *Asshole* to You." You walk into the used car dealership and up to the car you've been told to buy. When the salesperson approaches, you say the following: "You used car salespeople...I hate you! I want to spend as little time with you as I can. Here is the deal...you have 15 minutes to prove to me your costs in this car, what you paid for it, what repairs you made and for how much, and I'll pay you $400 above that amount, plus sales tax, that's it. That means $400 to you for 15 minutes work. Now that is the deal. 15 minutes, take it or leave it."

Here you have chosen a problem-solver's strategy with a competitive style. You appeal to your underlying goal: to spend no more than 15 minutes to reach a fair price. You appeal to the salesperson's underlying need, to get paid a fair price for their time. The style is in your face. It also depends on the dealer's willingness and ability to reveal their costs in a form that satisfies your requirements for proof.

Indeed, a choice should be made whether you should move from one approach to the other within the same negotiation. As with many aspects of negotiation, we intuitively make such moves. However, you will become a better negotiator by choosing to make the moves.

PROBLEM 1.1

Newman v. Popcheck

Plaintiff, Ms. Newman, was an attorney who had a dispute with her former law firm, and Mr. Popcheck, a senior partner in the firm. She alleges she was denied a bonus in the law firm because she was not friendly enough with Mr. Popcheck and that when he asked her out, to "calm her down," she refused, and was fired. She is seeking reinstatement and compensatory and punitive damages.

> Would you use an adversarial or problem-solving strategy in this negotiation?
>
> Would you use a competitive or cooperative style?
>
> Is there any additional information you need before you can answer these questions?

There is, of course, no one correct answer to these questions regarding representation of Ms. Newman. The problem is designed to start you thinking about the multitude of issues related to selection of an appropriate strategy or style. Looking at the strategy decision, an adversarial approach might work. After all, if a complaint has been filed asking for damages, you are dealing with a fungible item—money. To the extent plaintiff gets more, defendants have less. The risk of such an approach, however, is that if defense counsel takes an adversarial approach also, and their bargaining range does not overlap with plaintiff's bottom line, the parties may not agree. For example, if defendants want to pay no more than $75,000, but the plaintiff has decided she will accept no less than $250,000, there will be no agreement. Your decision to take an adversarial approach, therefore, must be premised, at least in part, on your confident expectation that the opposing side's bargaining range will overlap your bargaining range.

Also, if you represent the plaintiff, does one million dollars sought in the complaint adequately represent what your client wants out of the lawsuit? Through counseling have you determined that the dollar amount is less important than other intangible issues such as reputation, feelings of anger, or humiliation? Is the real issue not a fungible item at all? Or, does the client really want a combination of both money and social and psychological vindication? If the client's goals lean toward the latter, then you should take a creative problem-solving approach.

Of course, by starting out as a problem-solver, implying "there is more at stake than money," the plaintiff's attorney incurs two risks: revealing important information about the relative importance of money, and not getting as much money in the final deal. You might, therefore, start off as an adversarial negotiator, stake out a position, and then, using the techniques described in the chapters that follow gather sufficient information to determine if the defendant is willing to make a concession. If this strategy does not work, you might then shift to problem-solving. You might accomplish this shift to problem-solver by saying:

> PLAINTIFF'S ATTORNEY: Look, this doesn't appear to be working. Let me tell you, I need a break on this dollar amount. My client has to live until she gets a job with comparable earning potential. And let's be frank, there is no way that $50,000 sends the message that your clients are truly sorry about what occurred. Now I understand you can't break the

> firm, but let's see if there is some way to meet my client's needs as well as yours. What do you think? Is there some way this remorse can be communicated?

This example clearly communicates the need underlying the monetary position and invites a problem-solving approach in return. In response, defense counsel might offer to apologize. At that point, as plaintiff's counsel, you should pursue other solutions of this type, move on to other issues, or even return to the money issue by saying something like:

> Well that's a step in the right direction, but the dollar amount is still too low.

Of course, in a specific negotiation none of these scenarios may turn out to be the case. The point is, however, that whatever scenario unfolds it may be worth exploring the possibility of a creative, problem-solving solution.

The issue of style requires equally complex decisions. As a professional your immediate reaction may be to cooperate. After all, law has become a business and there is nothing to make you competitive. Indeed, long-term relationship issues may exist, at least for the lawyers. Are these lawyers you deal with on a regular basis? Do you rely on a good relationship to the benefit of your respective clients? If yes, the negotiation will naturally take on a cooperative tone.

The point is simply that you must consider the circumstances of the particular negotiation and consciously select the strategy and style best suited to the situation. Also, as with most choices you make, these choices need not—indeed, often should not—be immutable. As circumstances change, so might your strategy or style. One can easily imagine situations where you might want to start out as a competitive, aggressive individual. Imagine a situation where you represent a child in a short-term state psychiatric facility (average stay six weeks). You discover that your client, an emotionally disturbed 13 year old in the custody of social services, has been in this institution for two years. Your experts tell you that the child could function in a group home, and that, clearly contrary to state and federal law, the child has not been receiving an appropriate educational program.

In these circumstances, you could choose from either of two quite different courses. You could easily conclude that the long-term interests of this child require serious cooperative problem-solving by the very people who have apparently been ignoring the child for at least the past two years. Alternatively, you could just as easily conclude that trying to cooperate and problem-solve with people who have callously disregarded the child will be ineffective. You might, therefore, decide that the best approach is to start out as a competitive adversarial—threatening, perhaps even filing a lawsuit, calling for a meeting of lawyers and interested social service and educational providers, and communicating that you are angry and prepared to go to the mat for a client who has been ignored in the past. At some point, however, you would probably have to shift into a problem-solving approach to encourage the relevant service providers to think of creative ways to get the client the services he needs.

As a reminder of how strategy affects the language and stages of negotiation, at the end of each chapter we will provide a side-by-side chart that will describe these differences. The first one of these follows:

Language of Position Bargaining	Language of Problem-Solving
My offer is non-negotiable. I'm sorry, that is off the table. I'm not going to answer that. I moved last, it is your turn to counter. Is that your bottom line? I'll split the difference. Can we trade off on those two items?	Shall we first agree on a process that will lead to a fair resolution of the questions on the table? Help me understand why you take that position? What needs do you have and let's see if any of them are shared by both of us. I think there is a win-win solution in this for everyone. It might be most helpful for you to go first and tell me what you want and what your goals are. After I make sure I understand how you see it, then I'll tell you our point of view. Then we can brainstorm and see if there are any creative solutions we can come up with that are fair to each side's legitimate concerns, and yet produces the best solution for both sides.
Classic Stages of Position Bargaining	**Classic Stages of Interest Bargaining**
• Strategic icebreaking • Agenda bargaining • Questions and follow-up • Opening offers and persuasive statements • Concessions • Agreement or deadlock • If deadlock, subsequent offers and concessions till resolution • Write up and wrap up	• Icebreaking that is revealing, recognizes and respects the opponent, and evidences trust and goodwill • Exchange of full information, no blocks • Brainstorming—identifying all possible creative solutions • Identifying shared needs, independent needs, needs in conflict • Selecting best solution • Monitoring solution for fair implementation

Now that we have discussed the various strategies and styles of negotiators, the next chapter will introduce the various stages of a negotiation.

Eleven Stage Negotiati

(Assessment)

1. Preparation and p

2. Ice breaking

3. Agenda control

(Exchange and Asses:

4. Information bargai

5. Proposals, offers, d

Persuasion

6. Persuasion/justifica

(Assessment, Exchang

7. Concessions/reform

8. Crisis: resolution or

9. If deadlock: using mediator

10. Closing or wrap-u

11. Memorialization o

ıg may vary, but it virtually always

da setting. Fairly early in the pro-
what is subject to negotiation. Are
merger, settlement of a defamation
ations, or jury instructions? At this
th establishing how you will nego-
et the negotiation to move through
ı want them?

purpose of the negotiation, there is
on, often referred to as information
will seek information, reveal infor-
from each other.

g there typically follows a series of
:change. One party makes a proposal,
s a persuasive statement or justifica-
demand should be acceptable to the
ıt itself and counter proposals, offers,
o followed by a persuasive statement
ou are an adversarial negotiator) or
you are a problem-solver) then may
:curs; the point at which the parties
ons. It is here that the parties might
luator or neutral to help resolve areas
ws a closing and the agreement or lack
some manner, usually in writing.

ıts in the preface, you must recognize
ıework. In fact, viewing negotiation as
it is flexible. This framework's value is
ard manner the myriad of choices that
Once we understand that a face-to-face

The first stage of any nego hrough these stages, we can then alter
Whether you prepare for hours or combining stages.
into your office, most people give s
tion. In the preface it was pointed ustration of why this framework is only
in negotiation. Maximizing prepar es may have set the agenda by letter be-
ability to anticipate the choices th: Or, in a negligence action when plain-
                                     n to talk, both already know that the
Having done as much prepara, causation, and damages.
stage involves some type of interp

As another example, an important stage in the negotiation is the exchange of information. Although first in importance, it is not the first stage in a face-to-face negotiation. Many other things must first occur. In a given negotiation, however, you will choose to move the information exchange stage or major parts of it because of circumstances unique to that particular negotiation.

In a negligence action, serious negotiations to settle the case may not take place until after extensive formal and informal discovery. Counsel will obtain most of the historical facts of the action before the formal negotiation. Indeed, to wait until the face-to-face negotiation would be incompetency at its worst. But some information may be available only during settlement negotiations, given the state of the suit at that particular time, such as what are the real needs of the parties, economically, socially, and psychologically?

B. A Note on Plea Bargaining

Two types of plea bargaining take place in criminal proceedings. First, charge bargaining involves, as its name implies, negotiating over the crimes with which the defendant will be charged. Prosecutors have a wide range of crimes (burglary, grand larceny, breaking and entering, etc.) with which to charge a defendant found outside a home at night with a stereo in his hands. Charge bargaining involves negotiating which of these the prosecutor will charge the defendant with, and to which he ultimately pleads guilty. Second, sentence bargaining involves negotiating the sentence the prosecution will recommend the defendant receive in exchange for a guilty plea.

Within each of these types there will often be issues unrelated to either the specific crime charged or the sentence that will be received. For example, in negotiating a recommended sentence, the defendant may have authorized defense counsel to trade his testimony against a co-conspirator.

Recent statutory developments have made charge bargaining increasingly important. Mandatory minimum sentences and other sentencing guidelines often leave little discretion to the prosecutor if the focus is on sentence reduction.

Does any of this discussion of the stages of negotiation apply to plea bargaining? Yes. Prosecutors and defense counsel have the same variety of styles as do civil attorneys. Plea bargainers experience the same stages of the negotiating process as other negotiators. Criminal attorneys must prepare and plan. Prosecutors must choose the appropriate relationship with opposing counsel. Both negotiators agree on an agenda. Acquiring information concerning the strength of the prosecution's case is just as important to criminal defense counsel as the strength of plaintiff's case is to civil defense counsel.

Also, prosecutors and defense counsel come in various combinations of styles and strategies. Some defense counsel, for example, will be adversarial, staking out a position and viewing the process as a series of concessions and compromises: "My guy didn't do it and you can't prove it, but he wants to get this over with so he'll agree to the misdemeanor charge." Defense counsel are also just as likely to be problem-solvers: "Look, he's just a kid and needs help. The real problem is not that he shoplifted the goods; it's that he doesn't have the home structure he needs. How about we hold the charges and see if we can't get him into...."

There are, however, a number of factors that affect the plea bargaining process in a way that do not always affect transactional or civil litigation disputes. Two factors, for example, significantly affect information bargaining in plea negotiations. First, favoring the prosecution, is the fact that it has the resources of the state at its disposal. While clearly the state does not always choose to overwhelm the defendant with these resources, the fact remains that the state, if it so chooses, can outspend almost all defendants. Second, favoring the defendant, is that in most jurisdictions discovery in criminal actions clearly favors the defendant, with the prosecutor having a greater responsibility for turning over evidence than the defendant.

C. Transactional Bargaining

Transactional lawyers are most often bargaining about the language in documents. For example, in a merger, it seems that the investment bankers have had all the fun in setting the price, and all the lawyers do is slow down the process and think of reasons why the parties ought not do the deal.

One might think that because transactional lawyers represent buyers and sellers who are selling tangible items that they would most likely be adversarial position bargainers. They would be drawn to the tactics of the "bazaar" and haggle until they move each other into a range of settlement. Deal lawyers, however, while worried about value and risk, are also worried about control. Moreover, most deals require some ongoing relationship. At a minimum, payment may be made over a period of time and depend on its success on the future viability of the new business. So, like other bargainers, transactional lawyers need an ability to Problem-solve: to understand the underlying goals of the language of the deals they are drafting in order to know when to fight about the language, or think creatively in order to draft in a way that each side wins. Transaction lawyers must remember the mantra of deal makers during the negotiation of the deal: *The person who understands the deal controls the deal.* This is true whether the fight is about tax formulations, representations and warranties, management structure, or contingent liabilities. Where deal lawyers and litigators have more in common than they think is when they plan for and conduct negotiations.

In addition, transactional bargainers must understand that the parties may not have enough information at the time of the closing to value later risks. In these situations they might draw on evaluative or meditative processes to solve the disputes when they arise. They must think ahead to the litigation that might arise in the future, and lay out a process now that will fairly resolve different later-arising disputes.

With this general overview we will now turn to a detailed discussion of each of the stages. As we discuss each stage, keep in mind that we will want to identify not only what we need to do, but how we do it. We also want to ask ourselves whether how we do it differs depending on which style and strategy we use.

CHAPTER 3
THE SOCIAL PSYCHOLOGY
OF NEGOTIATION

Researchers have long recognized that a social/psychological dynamic permeates all stages of the negotiation process. This "social psychology" can have a significant impact on the negotiation. Our personal observations confirm the fact that people do things in a negotiation for reasons other than a rational business or economic judgment. If you can identify these potential pressures, you can then use them to help "persuade" the person with whom you are negotiating to accept your proposal. Also important, if you recognize these other pressures at work on you, you can choose to either allow yourself to be influenced by them or let them influence the negotiation.

Social psychological pressures occur in a variety of circumstances. The Dollar Auction game makes a number of these points. Ask a group of lawyers to participate in a dollar auction with the following rules, and watch what happens:

Dollar Auction

—First bid greater than 50c.

—At least 5c increments.

—You owe me your last bid.

Routinely you will get an opening bid at fifty-five cents. Or sometimes someone will bid ninety-five cents. But low and behold, the auctioneer can get another bid at one-hundred cents. It is at this point that the group becomes aware of the real meaning of the last rule: You owe me your last bid. Often then, in order to save face, the other bidders will bid more than a dollar for the dollar. It becomes a matter of winning the dollar, rather than whether it makes sense to bid as much as they bid. When the bidding stalls the auctioneer can often provoke higher bids by:

❖ Interviewing the bidders and getting personal information out to the group that may raise the embarrassment factor

❖ Simply telling the bidder that they *really need* another bid to make a point

Whenever the Dollar Auction is played with these moves the psychological affect on the audience is quite palpable and predictable. The audience tends to look at the auctioneer with suspicion. They feel tricked. Yet they recognize that what has happened is not that far removed from a typical litigation setting negotiation.

The audience learns about sunk costs: that a party is willing to spend more than a dollar for a dollar because if they give up bargaining they will lose all they have already invested in the outcome. To avoid losing what they have already invested for nothing, they are willing to pay even more to get something. This is the analytical and economic lesson of the auction. The other lessons are psychological and social.

We are all familiar with situations where a person has taken a position that can only be justified by their desire to "save face." With perhaps more worthy motivations you may recall situations where you or another person in the negotiation "gave" the other side a concession because you "wanted to be nice" or "to avoid a fight." The lawyer who agrees to a day off for a member of the staff because she likes the staff member may have an economic motivation (keeping a good employee happy), but the lawyer also may just feel good by waiving a policy that might otherwise prohibit the day off.

Organizations are also subject to social psychological pressures. We sometimes read in the newspapers about the social and psychological aspects of major negotiations. One need only read about a bank, or any other business merger, in which the two entities are going to combine names, or create an entirely new name. Certainly combining the two names may have an economic justification—taking advantage of name recognition—but people involved in these types of negotiations will also tell you that combining names provides a soothing compromise for people with an emotional attachment to the original name.

A review of some of the more common social psychological influences will illustrate how these pressures work to facilitate or inhibit acceptance of an opponent's particular position.

A. Audiences to the Negotiation

Researchers point out that an audience can significantly impact a negotiation. By audience we do not mean simply that someone may be in the room watching the negotiation. By audience it is meant that someone somewhere is observing directly or indirectly the negotiation or its results.

The types of audiences are quite broad. They run from the obvious— "the folks back home for whom you are negotiating," or a colleague sitting in on the negotiation—to the more subtle—your spouse when you discuss your day at the office. Audiences to a negotiation involving a lawyer include, for example:

❖ the lawyer's supervisors or superiors;

❖ the lawyer's professional peers, colleagues, co-workers;

❖ the lawyer's spouse;

❖ the current client in whose interest the lawyer is negotiating;

❖ other clients;

❖ potential clients.

Psychologists tell us that the existence of an audience motivates negotiators to seek positive evaluations from the audience. This is common sense. No one wants to go back to the office and reveal to his or her colleagues that they have just made the worst agreement of the year.

Of course, different audiences will evaluate a negotiation differently. A supervising partner may evaluate the associate-bargainer from a profitability (to the firm) and quality standpoint. Did the lawyer get a good deal in a difficult negotiation? The client might evaluate the bargainer in light of factors such as speed or profitability to them (as opposed to the firm). The one common denominator, however, is that if the negotiator is accountable to an audience, this accountability provides a means to control the negotiator.

In blunt terms, if you can give the negotiator what an influential audience desires, you can manipulate the lawyer to accept what the audience wants, as opposed to perhaps what the lawyer wants. The clearest example of this, of course, is the client as audience. In our defamation action for Ms. Newman, we will spend a great deal of time trying to figure out what the audience/client really wants. If you can figure out what the client wants, more likely than not, the desires of the lawyer with whom you are negotiating become irrelevant. Give the lawyer what the client wants and the lawyer should ultimately go along.

PROBLEM 3.1

Refer to Problem 1.1, where plaintiff's lawyer is negotiating with defendant, the law firm Popcheck et al. Plaintiff alleges sexual harassment.

> What audiences would there be for the negotiation?

> How, if at all, would your overall strategy of the negotiation be affected by those audiences?

> Is there any additional information you need before you can definitely answer these questions?

The client is not the only audience. For example, in Problem 3.1 defendants Popcheck Blink & Denis have an audience that consists of other law firms. If plaintiff, Newman, can identify how Popcheck, et al views that audience, the plaintiff's attorney can use that information to his or her advantage. For example, is the existence of the lawsuit generally known in the legal community? If not, the threat of continuing the suit and risking exposure with a resultant loss of prestige may have considerable influence on the negotiation and the firm's willingness to settle. If the existence of the suit is already generally known, this knowledge could conceivably make settlement harder. For example, the defendants may feel that to settle the case will have a significantly negative impact on the firm's reputation if a settlement is interpreted as an admission of liability. The reputation of the firm may be better served by going to trial and suffering a defeat than to admit responsibility. Putting together an acceptable settlement package under these circumstances will be particularly difficult if plaintiff's own goals include seeking precisely the kind of public recognition of liability that the firm seeks to avoid.

As with all aspects of the negotiation process, the pressure of an audience must also be evaluated from the negotiator's perspective. The negotiator who has the audience must try to avoid being manipulated by that audience. For example, a common question for lawyers is whether the client should attend the actual face-to-face negotiation with the opposing counsel. As with most issues related to negotiation, there is no one right answer. This audience dynamic, however, is certainly an important consideration in deciding whether the client should be present.

In a negotiation involving a business transaction that requires a high level of technical expertise, there is often little question that having a client with that expertise attend could be helpful. The value of that expertise must, however, be weighed against the fact that opposing counsel will have direct access to your most important audience. If the client is unable to control his or her reactions to opposing counsel's negotiation ploys, you may be at a serious disadvantage.

It should be quickly added that the cooperative problem-solver must be as aware of these dynamics as the competitive adversarial. For example, lawyers are constantly subject to scrutiny by colleagues. Human nature being what it is, the lawyer probably prefers to be respected by his or her colleagues as opposed to being held in low esteem. If the general wisdom among opposing counsel's colleagues values aggressive negotiations, the lawyer will likely behave accordingly. Recognizing this, the competitive adversarial should take steps to avoid exacerbating that characteristic. The cooperative problem-solving defense attorney should probably try to avoid plea bargaining with the competitive adversarial prosecutor in the hallways of the court where other prosecutors or police officers are present.

B. Restraints on Communication

Researchers also tell us that restrictions on communication can have a significant impact on the negotiation. These restrictions may be either between the negotiators or between the negotiator and the negotiator's own people. For example, communication isolation imposes constraints on the development of cooperation and promotes distrust and suspicion. A party who is unable to contact her own support group (colleagues, supervisor, secretary) may be more distrustful.

The lesson seems obvious that if you are dealing with a person who is generally distrustful to begin with when trying to work out a joint venture, it may be to your advantage to ensure that this type of isolation does not occur. You might propose meeting at the other lawyer's or other client's place of business. Or, if you meet at your office, try to ensure your counterpart has frequent opportunities to take breaks and use the telephone privately.

PROBLEM 3.2

Assume you are a lawyer for Ms. Newman in the sexual harassment action mentioned in Problem 1.1. You wish to set up a meeting to discuss possible settlement with counsel for Popcheck Blink & Denis. You have now called three times leaving messages. The attorney for Popcheck Blink & Denis has returned your calls twice, but you have been out of the office.

> How is Popcheck Blink & Denis's attorney likely to feel?

> How would you feel under these circumstances?

> What steps might you take to deal with the communication problem?

> Does the communication problem give you any insight into other aspects of the negotiation?

Restrictions on verbal communication between negotiators also can have a negative impact on the process. When verbal communication is eliminated effectiveness often suffers. All too frequently this occurs when you play telephone tag with someone. As your frustration develops over your inability to contact a lawyer, your anxiety or anger may increase, making it less likely that you will develop the relationship necessary to complete the deal. It may seem obvious, but using a letter at this point can be extremely helpful. Likewise, voice mail is underutilized as a means not just of leaving a message requesting a call in return, but actually to engage in a discussion by leaving a detailed message outlining needs, interests, and the like. Leaving a message that the lawyer should return your call at a specific time when you will be in your office, can be very effective.

Keep in mind that if you feel frustration and anger, the other person may be feeling it as well. Directly confronting this may help maintain or develop an appropriate relationship.

C. Respect and Anger

One of the most difficult emotional forces at work that prevents conflict resolution, and, in fact may escalate the conflict is anger. The experience of a dollar auction often proves this. When a person feels isolated and embarrassed, they may become angry and just "shut down" and say nothing and refuse to move.

To see how this is so, think first about a conflict that arises between a parent and child, and how it informs our understanding of disputes, generally.

Imagine being the parent of a fifteen-year-old daughter. You, your wife, and your other children are all waiting for the arrival of your fifteen-year-old daughter, so that you can leave on your long anticipated family vacation. You are making the trip by car, and need to leave at 4:00 p.m. to be able to stop for dinner and arrive at your cottage by 10:00 p.m. When your daughter left that morning for the last day of school, you made sure she knew to be home from school by 4:00 p.m. so that you could leave on time. Your last words to her were, "Don't be late." Now it is 4:30 p.m., and still no daughter. Might your anger be on the rise?

Conflict resolution theorists tell us that what is likely to happen next is a problem inherent in the coming together of anger and feelings of lack of respect. What is likely is that you will attribute a motive to your daughter's lateness that may produce a significant long-standing effect on your relationship with your daughter and your ability to resolve your conflict with her.

Imagine that when she shows up you let your anger take over. You might even yell and scream at her for her behavior. You will likely attribute her behavior to lack of respect for you and the family. You might even further attribute her behavior to a character defect she has, that she is inconsiderate, routinely late, and self-centered. These are character traits that come from you (or her mother), and you were afraid they would surface in her, and now they have and she has this flaw in her character.

She gets angry and cries. She says she was with her friends and has a right to be! She says you are too compulsive, and what difference does it make if we get the to cottage a few minutes later. She says that she is afraid of you, and that you can't control your temper. That she hates you and hates living in this family. She runs into her room, slams the door, and locks it.

What is likely to happen is what conflict resolution theorists' describe as the volatile combination of attribution error and anger.[4] Attribution is the process whereby a harmdoer and the harmed party assign responsibility for the harmdoer's behavior. Each confronts the other with their judgment about who is responsible for the harm. The judgment of responsibility turns on the nature of the harmdoer's excuses and motives for causing the harm.

What conflict resolution theorists tell us next is of utmost importance. They tell us that they can predict how anger and loss of respect lead to predictable judgments about the appropriate responsibility that the injuring party will bear. The common judgments of appropriate responsibility can be safely laid out as follows:

❖ Intentional harmful behavior: leads to an apology, punishment, and the need to repay a fair amount;

❖ Negligent harmful behavior: leads to a different kind of apology and a change in behavior over those things the harmdoer can fairly control, as well fair compensation;

❖ Excusable harmful behavior: leads to no apology and no compensation.

Where, however, the judgment of appropriate responsibility is at odds with the injuring party's feelings, the following are the likely effects on the parties:

---

4   Keith G. Allred, ANGER AND RETALIATION IN CONFLICT: THE ROLE OF ATTRIBUTION, in eds. Morton Deutsch & Peter T. Coleman, THE HANDBOOK OF CONFLICT RESOLUTION: THEORY AND PRACTICE, 236-245, (2000).

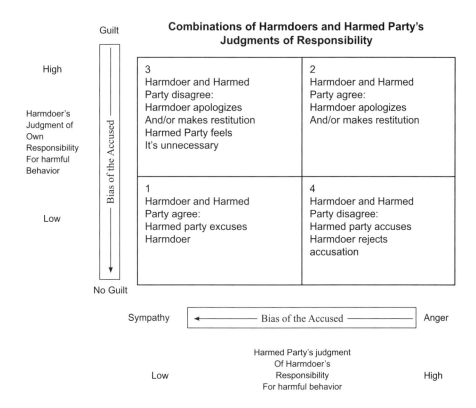

Combinations of Harmdoers and Harmed Party's Judgments of Responsibility

Guilt

High

Harmdoer's
Judgment of
Own
Responsibility
For harmful
Behavior

Low

No Guilt

3
Harmdoer and Harmed
Party disagree:
Harmdoer apologizes
And/or makes restitution
Harmed Party feels
It's unnecessary

2
Harmdoer and Harmed
Party agree:
Harmdoer apologizes
And/or makes restitution

1
Harmdoer and Harmed
Party agree:
Harmed party excuses
Harmdoer

4
Harmdoer and Harmed
Party disagree:
Harmed party accuses
Harmdoer rejects
accusation

Bias of the Accused

Sympathy ← —— Bias of the Accused —— Anger

Low

Harmed Party's judgment
Of Harmdoer's
Responsibility
For harmful behavior

High

Of course most of the time there is some combination of behavior or there is a disagreement about the nature of the excuses and whether they are controllable.

Consider for example how differently you feel about the family trip situation when your daughter reports the following story: She was approached by a good friend in tears who asked for her help. Her friend's stepfather was approaching her sexually, and she wanted some help about what to do. She did not know where to turn and wanted your daughter to talk to her and help her figure out what best to do.

Do you see what has happened? A paradigm shift has just occurred.[5] It is inappropriate for you to have been angry, because your daughter's excuse relates to circumstances beyond her control. You would have been disappointed in her if she had not taken the time to talk to her friend. (You might have preferred for her to have called and explained the situation, but still you do not blame her, nor is it fair to attribute responsibility to her that would require the same level of apol-

---

5   Steven Covey, SEVEN HABITS OF HIGHLY EFFECTIVE PEOPLE, Habit 5, where Covey argues that effective people should try not to react in anger, but seek first to understand, before being understood. He otherwise refers to this habit as the habit of "courageous compassion." See, Stephen R. Covey, PRINCIPLED-CENTERED LEADERSHIP, 45, (1992).

ogy, punishment, and compensation that you and she might otherwise feel is appropriate.)

Moreover, there is more at stake here. Because of your anger, you have attributed her behavior to disrespect at best, self-centeredness, and, more likely, an intentional motive to harm the family. These attribution errors can cause the most damage to the ability of the parties to resolve the conflict. If the parties are not able to fairly assess what excuses are really available, and whether they are beyond the control of the harmdoer, the parties are likely to attribute the behavior to intent, disrespect, and character flaws, provoking not guilt, but a righteous sense of being wronged, harmed, and unfairly blamed. These feelings will likely provoke an escalating angry response, as you gave in your reaction.

These are the same feelings that are in play when an opponent bargainer refuses to return phone calls, laughs at your opening offer, rejects out of hand your client's injury, stereotypes your client along with fakers, or all uncaring arrogant institutions.

While these psychological forces operate between the parties, they can also operate between the lawyers. How often does a lawyer get angry during a negotiation? How often is anger a result of the lawyer perceiving that her opponent or client does not respect either the lawyer or lawyer's client? The lawyer attributes the behavior of the opponent and/ or opponent's representative to an intention to harm, or to a character flaw in the opponent/client, or industry they represent. When anger occurs, the negotiators tend to say things that attribute the worst motives to their opposition and that are destructive to dispute resolution. They attribute greed and disrespect to the harmdoer or to the harmed party. Their lawyers tend to exaggerate the dispute by taking extreme positions. Then their opponents can point to these exaggerations as evidence of the lawyer's lying. As a result they justify tactics that obfuscate, deny responsibility, and justify taking further extreme positions because of the fear that any admission will be used to unfairly punish and exact retribution. Conflict escalates and can lead to deadlock, unless cooler heads prevail.

What does it mean in this context for cooler heads to prevail? The lawyer must think strategically for ways to deal with his or her own anger, and think strategically for ways to deal with the opponent's anger. The first problem is one that is related to self control, and can be managed very much like any self-control issue. Like an addiction, the problem with anger is that, to some, it feels good, it is born of an instinct to fight, is related to adrenalin, and feelings of power, and, for some, is very hard to control. For the lawyer, it is often confused with the legitimate role that the lawyer must play to passionately and zealously represent their clients within the bounds of law.

Because our opponents may be cowered by anger and "flee" rather than fight if they think the anger is irrational enough, the effect may be that the negotiator's anger accomplishes the goal: an outcome in his client's favor. After all, for a threat to be effective, it must be heard, understood, and believed. The emotion and passion of the speaker communicate a willingness to back up his position with violence, if necessary, and, at times, aid in the "believability" part of making a threat effective.

At risk, however, are escalation, deadlock, and permanent damage to the relationship. Interestingly, expressing a position in anger may make one more wedded to it, and less willing to see the weakness in the position. In addition, a skilled opponent may see anger as weakness, not strength, and related to the flight instinct. They may also see the failure of self control as a character flaw, indicating lack of confidence in the client's position. The lawyer needs to be able to understand anger and manage it in order to implement the client's goals.

First, the lawyer must recognize that he is feeling angry, and the reactive effect of this behavior. With this self knowledge in hand the lawyer can plan for what to do if the feeling of anger arises, including using role plays and developing habits to better control the anger. Some suggest that an effective way to manage anger is to develop a self-regulatory plan and implementation strategy. Just as a smoker who is trying to quit might plan what to do when he or she craves a smoke, so the lawyer might create a plan for when he starts to feel angry. The more specific the plan, the better your chance of overcoming the feeling. For example, a lawyer might create a plan as follows: 1) when the opponent's lawyer accuses me of being unreasonable in my demand for damages, I will cite specific recent decisions and settlements of similar size. 2) I will say to myself, this little mantra, "Do not get angry. Anger is not helpful, and will harm the client." 3) If the opponent rejects those cases and refuses to discuss them because my client was negligent, recognize the tactic as a position bargaining tactic, and not a personal affront. Plan, instead, to ask the opponent to place probabilities on the jury finding a fact in the opponent's favor, and if the opponent refuses, plan to write down your own probability to keep yourself more analytical and less emotional.

As with addiction management, anger management has steps. It involves recognition of the feeling and the development of a mantra. It often gives the person something physical to do; like writing down what you will do next, or writing what you will say before you say it, or playing with a piece of tape. In addition it provides for a backup. In other words, when the feelings are very powerful, give yourself some place to go (take a break), or something else to talk about, or someone else to talk to or involve in the process.[6]

When the negotiator sees anger in his or her opponent, the negotiator can also plan what to do. Naming it (saying that your opponent is angry), and taking a time out, are common effective strategies. Examining your own behavior to determine whether you might have unfairly caused the anger, and apologizing, is also a very good place to start.[7]

Experiences with adversarial bargaining have caused conflict resolution theorists to start devising a better model for conducting negotiations resolving conflicts. And the problem-solver provides a way of turning a deadlock into a process.

A problem-solving model seeks to create a set of negotiating steps and procedures that will better control the biasing effects on client decision making, and better control the social and psychological forces that lead to deadlock. It also tries to provide a different, more creative strategy to devise more particularized creative solutions.

Problem-solving attempts to learn from psychiatry. Psychiatrists recommend that counselors, negotiators, and mediators seek to listen for understanding before attempting to persuade in order to keep emotions from biasing the decision making. Important to resisting the adversarial role-playing involved in most position bargaining would be for the problem-solver to instead initially serve the role as "listener."[8] The need for true understanding is a threshold for any connectedness

---

6   Walter Mishel and Aaron L. DeSmet, SELF-REGULATION IN THE SERVICE OF CONFLICT RESOLUTION, in Morton Deutsch and Peter T. Coleman, THE HANDBOOK OF CONFLICT RESOLUTION, 269-270, (2000).

7   Keith G. Allred, ANGER AND RETALIATION IN CONFLICT, in Morton Deutsch and Peter T. Coleman, THE HANDBOOK OF CONFLICT RESOLUTION, 246 (2000).

8   Professor Zwier was first introduced to the role of "listener" by Maude Pervere and Janeen Kerper, at a planning conference held by the National Institute for Trial Advocacy for developing a new program for lawyers to reimagine the lawyer client relationship. Pervere and Kerper then referred us to Tom Rusk's work, THE POWER OF ETHICAL PERSUASION, (1993) (Hereinafter Rusk). Rusk is a noted psychiatrist who has been instrumental in developing models for teaching community mediation.

and necessary empathy, and is best described in the work of psychiatrist Tom Rusk, *The Power of Ethical Persuasion*. He writes,

> It's mysterious and ironic that after millions of years of evolution—and a hundred or so of modern psychological theorizing and research—we humans have not advanced very far in person-to-person communications. We can generally exchange thoughts and ideas pretty well, but nonetheless we often fail to understand each other. For the most part, what we fail to communicate clearly is our feelings, those nonverbal, deeply rooted energies that can lead us to act in contradiction to our will and our rational decisions. Between people, strong feelings can easily escalate a simple misunderstanding into a senseless battle of wills. Even wars between nations have begun that way.

> Modern psychology has done relatively little to help us comprehend our feelings, or learn to manage them in understanding, caring, and fairness in order to create happier, more fulfilling lives. (Emphasis in the original.) Many successful books on communication strategies have sought to teach people how to expedite problem-solving or gain the upper hand in all kinds of negotiations. But these strategies almost always ignore the power of feelings in all kinds of relationships, and the need to uphold explicit social values in the conduct of human communication.

> As far as I'm concerned, there never was or will be a better basic communication strategy than the Golden Rule: Do unto others as you would have them do unto you. Ethical persuasion is a practical, strategic method of applying the Golden Rule to every kind of important communication—not as a means of merely doing a "good deed," but as a means of giving everyone a fair hearing, creating the optimal solutions for thorny problems, and fostering long-term, trusting relationships.

Rusk's listening techniques then correspond with the techniques that Mnookin describes in his book, *Beyond Winning: Negotiation to Create Value in Deals and Disputes*, and Fisher and Ury describe in their book, *Getting to Yes*. Rusk's ethical persuasion is the practical "how to" for the moral philosophy of persuasion. Rusk describes seven steps to good listening.

1. Establish that your immediate goal is mutual understanding, not problem-solving.

2. Elicit the other person's thoughts, feelings, and desires about the subject at hand.

3. Ask for the other person's help in understanding him or her. Try not to defend or disagree.

4. Repeat the other person's position in your own words to show you understand.

5. Ask the other person to correct your understanding and keep restating his or her position.

6. Refer back to your position only to keep things going.

7. Repeat steps 1-6 until the other person unreservedly agrees that you understand his or her position.[9]

Listening then is a key to understanding and understanding is key to solving problems within the moral orientation that takes feelings into account, but does not provide them with unfair, or bias effects. Listening should be done first because it will help break the lawyer out of position bargaining role playing. It establishes the lawyer in the learning mode first, as opposed to the doing mode. It subverts what the lawyer knows to what the opponent knows and feels. In addition, to the extent that information is power, the listener has the advantage of knowing both sides (lawyer's and the opponent's) before speaking. In addition, listening earns the listener the leverage of fairness. The more the opponent is listened to and understood, the more the opponent will likely listen and seek understanding in return. Finally these seven steps cultivate in the listener patience and openness which are behaviors that evidence respect.[10]

Again, Rusk has some concrete practical advice for the negotiator during the third step when the lawyer may express his position in the matter. Rusk's steps better ensure that the advocate is acting out of respect. Rusk describes these as follows:[11]

---

9   Rusk, *supra*, note 53, at 7–8.

10 *Id.* at 69–70.

11 *Id.* at 89.

1. Ask for a fair hearing in return.

2. Begin with an explanation of how the other person's thoughts and feelings affect you. Avoid blaming and self-defense as much as possible.

3. Carefully explain your thoughts, desires, and feelings as your truth, not the truth.

4. Ask for restatements of your position—and corrections of any factual inaccuracies—as necessary.

5. Review your respective positions.

The result is that the win/lose, "I'm right and you are wrong," dichotomy may immediately be broken. The possible solutions that arise multiply greatly when the focus turns to what will create, maintain or maximize the healthy relationships already present in the situation. Within a relationship of trust and respect, each negotiator will look for ways for each side to win. In fact, as we will explore in further chapters, this active listening and advanced empathy may be the negotiator bridge between position bargaining and problem-solving.

D. Social Psychology of Selected Tactics

Many standard negotiating techniques have psychological overtones. Several of the more common are worth addressing here.

1. Timing Ploys

A common negotiating technique is to set a deadline by which agreement must be met. This tactic often works. As time pressures increase, bargaining aspirations, demands, and the amount of bluffing tends to decrease.

2. Overly Demanding and Other Biases

Some research has shown that perceptions of one side being demanding, resisting, or unjust, correlates with the other side raising intangible issues of honor, public image, face, and self-esteem. And it raises the broader question that challenges economic analysis of bargaining. Why do the parties not act rationally and agree on questions of value?

Some have argued that position bargaining also fails to produce creative, particularized, and lasting solutions between the parties.[12] They argue that a different strategy for negotiation is needed: one that makes joint problem-solvers out of the negotiators in order that the parties will better resolve their dispute.

Let's look more closely at the psychology of each party in the decision-making process to determine how to think differently and strategically about the case.

Cognitive psychologists, especially the *behaviorists*, caution that even professional decision makers are not as rational as one might expect (especially as defined by optimal efficiency principals). The parties might value their cases differently because one is more naïve and intuitive, or is susceptible to error or ideological bias. Or, one side's client or lawyer is just simply not very skilled at case valuation or counseling. They are stuck in the warrior mode, and miss the keys to case valuation and settlement.

Professor Lagevoort describes cognitive psychological literature on decision-making biases and advises lawyers to take an interest in behavioral psychology as it affects decision making and may inhibit optimal conflict resolution.[13] This literature suggests that non-rational biases come in seven forms:

Status Quo/Loss Aversion Biases and Framing Effects

This bias is noted as a decision maker's preference for risk aversion and a natural bias for the status quo.

Anchoring and Adjustment

People tend to "anchor" on some initial possibility in decision-making, and fail to adjust carefully as new information becomes available.

Illusory Correlations and Causation Biases

Clients often find causal patterns and relationships in matters that are the product of random chance.

Biases in Risk Perception

Clients seem to ignore low risk factors that have not been made salient, or seem to value uncertainty differently at the extremes. They

---

12 Robert H. Mnookin, Beyond Winning: Negotiation to Create Value in Deals and Disputes, (2000). Fisher & Ury, Getting to Yes (1981).

13 Donald C. Lagevoort, Symposium: The Legal Implications of Psychology: Human Behavior, Behavioral Economics, and the Law: Behavioral Theories of judgment and Decision Making in Legal Scholarship.

tend to ignore risk differences in the 5%–10% category, and place more significance on removing the 5% and less risk of a bad thing happening.

The Hindsight Bias

People overestimate their fault when they could have predicted the outcome, and the outcome happens.

Context Bias

Relative preference between two possible outcomes may bias someone against a compromise as a third outcome.

Intertemporal Biases

There is a bias toward consumption and against deferred gratification.

Egocentric Biases

Self-serving construals, explaining successes by reference to efficiency and control, and failures to reference luck, or other external circumstances that contributed to their gains.

Of course, not only are clients affected by these biases, but so, also, are their lawyers. Lawyers then tend to think of negotiation as an opportunity to persuade the opposing party, not only as to the predicted value of the cases as a matter of economics, but also to "bias" the decision in their favor by persuading the other side as a matter of psychology. Focus groups and mock trials can greatly aid in this process as they may provide the empirical correction necessary for the biasing effects on the various decision makers.

The problems with lawyers taking a solely economic valuation view of negotiation—discovering expected values at trial, in the light of traditional court decisions—are twofold. One, it ignores the social psychology inherent in dispute resolution, and two, that courts, most often, are stuck with a win-lose decision. One party wins and one loses. Seldom is the court able to customize a particularized solution to the parties' problem. Those solutions are left to the parties both before and after the court reaches its decision. And it is very difficult for a litigator not to think in win/lose, "zero-sum game" terms.

PROBLEM 3.3

Green v. Hall and Rose. You are in negotiations with a real estate broker and her client concerning their refusal of your black client's offer to buy in favor of the offer of a white client. The buyer says the white buyer's offer was higher, and that she was under no obligation to accept the first bid. The black buyers say that their offer was turned down without their being given an opportunity to counter offer. They say it is customary and common courtesy to give a buyer the opportunity to raise their offer.

The real estate broker has begun to take the steps necessary to promote better communication of offers between prospective buyers and sellers in order to ensure that racial discrimination does not take place. Your clients want to make sure that this does not happen again. In addition, your clients want the owner to pay an amount in retribution for the way they were treated.

What overall strategy should you use in this negotiation?

What style should you use?

In some circumstances, you must be careful not to come on "too strong," particularly where the expected response from those with whom you are negotiating is that they fear a public loss of status or control. Under these circumstances, the opposing negotiator may make a "strategic" decision that regardless of the ultimate outcome, he or she must make a public show of opposition in order to maintain that public perception.

There are psychological issues at work between agent bargainers, as well as between clients. To some, these psychological forces overwhelm the analytical ones, and make conflict resolution a fundamentally nonrational, if not irrational process. They prefer position-bargaining strategies to deal with social psychological issues. Others would rather use cooperative strategies to provide each side with a better understanding of the other's point of view. They argue that the conflict resolution process is dependent instead on building trust and building a relationship between the parties so that they choose to agree rather than fight.

Furthermore, the adversarial position-bargaining strategies used by lawyers can exacerbate feelings of mistrust and competition.

How this will play out depends on the specific circumstances. For example, assume you are negotiating with the broker and use the owner's racist comments ascribing intentional wrongdoing to the broker. If your only goal is to get the broker to do a better job of communicating with and on behalf of prospective buyers, attributing racist motives to the broker is likely to provoke a deadlock. The injustice of a wrong attribution of motive can jeopardize the goal. Problem-solving will be at a premium.

Your client, however, may have other goals in mind besides punishing the broker. They may want to also put the whole issue behind them. If the client wants to expose a pattern of behavior, you might make public demands while recognizing that in the short term it will make the broker more likely to resist. As with everything associated with negotiation, no one right way exists; there are only choices given the circumstances of the particular negotiation. Also, your history with the broker might be such that you know that regardless of which approach you take, the broker will react aggressively and that ultimately you will have "to go public" to put additional pressure on the broker. It all depends.

3. Deference Toward Authority

In general human interaction, bargainers display considerable deference toward high, or higher, status people by frequent compliance with their threats and by submissive behavior. For example, if you as a supervisor meet a subordinate in the cafeteria and say you would like to meet at 3:00 p.m., the employee likely will come to your office at 3:00 p.m. He or she will have deferred to a higher authority.

PROBLEM 3.4

In your position at work what steps can you take
to establish that you are the higher authority?

Many different things create the authority or the impression of authority that can work in response to Problem 3.4. As you look around your practice setting, what things indicate authority or lack of authority? Titles clearly do. Bankers have long recognized the importance of titles and use the title of vice president quite liberally to create the impression of authority. Are such titles present in your work environment? Compare the title of staff attorney versus associate general counsel.

Physical environment can also create the impression of authority. Do you negotiate in a cubicle or in a formal conference room? Two very different impressions can result. Similarly, dress can help establish authority. Why do physicians wear white coats in the hospital even when not performing clinical roles? Status and authority are communicated.

Perhaps most importantly, what does your negotiating behavior say about your authority? Do you need a supervising attorney to approve every action? Has an agreement you have reached been re-evaluated by a supervisor, who then required that you seek changes?

4. Extreme Demands

In negotiations that reach agreement, bargainers generally attain higher and more satisfactory outcomes when they begin with extreme rather than more moderate demands. This makes sense when you recognize that one of the primary problems associated with negotiation is not having sufficient information to know the strength of your position. When you buy a car you usually do not have sufficient information to know whether your offer is too high or too low. Anyone who has bought a house knows the fear of the seller accepting your first offer and your own reaction or feeling that if they accepted the first offer it was too high. We will discuss in detail how to avoid this situation through a systematic approach to negotiation. You should always keep in mind that when in doubt, ask for more rather than less.

Of course, a risk is associated with extreme demands. While an extreme demand may result in more if settlement is reached, an extreme demand may increase the perception of a lack of willingness to negotiate seriously and therefore increase the risk of deadlock.

5. Allowing Yourself to Be Persuaded

Another important social/psychological factor at work in negotiations is that a bargainer wants to believe he is capable of shaping the other's behavior—of causing the other to choose as he does. Therefore, you might occasionally want to tell the person with whom you are negotiating that they have persuaded you on certain issues. This may in turn create a more favorable relationship between the two of you.

6. Promises and Threats

If a bargainer believes he cannot successfully exert influence in other ways, he may revert to promises and threats. Threats result quite often from a negotiator's feeling of frustration and inability to develop more constructive approaches. If you supervise other people, think back to when you have had to threaten disciplinary action if the person did not change their behavior. Most likely, the threat was the result of frustration that other, more constructive, actions failed. When you feel the pressure to threaten, or when you are threatened, your first thought should be that the threat is in reality a warning. The threat is a warning that you should redouble efforts to try to find more constructive actions.

The need to find alternative approaches in the face of threats is critical because the use of threats decreases the likelihood of a mutually favorable result. Once again, this is common sense. When you are threatened, what is your usual response? Are you more likely to give in, or fight on regardless of the cost?

Merely identifying that these things occur is not enough. You must be prepared to identify their likely occurrence in a particular negotiation and plan how to either use them to your advantage or minimize their impact. Take threats, for example. If you believe the person you will negotiate with will likely use threats, and it will negatively impact the negotiation, prepare to respond accordingly. The appropriate response requires you to ask why people make threats. Typically, they make them because they have nothing else to use to get you to comply. Your first step may be to ensure that the negotiation takes a more principled approach, providing a more meaningful way of discussing problems. Your second step is to deal directly with the threat, by asking what would make a threat effective and then diffusing these items. How to do this is discussed in Chapter 7, the Exchange.

D. Gender Differences

Women who negotiate on a regular basis often report that women are treated differently by men in negotiations compared to the way their male counterparts are treated. Reports that women are subject to more attempts to intimidate are not uncommon. Women also report that they seem to approach the negotiation differently than men. Is there any truth to these anecdotal reports? Research indicates there may be some truth to these perceptions, though the data are mixed.

Professor Gerald Williams has reported that, based on his empirical research, people do not change their approach to negotiation based on the sex of the opposing party.[14] Men who are cooperative in one setting typically are cooperative in all settings. This does not mean, however, that the perceptions reported by so many women are wrong. What this means, Williams theorizes, is that aggressive individuals are aggressive in all settings. Therefore, some men will make sexually demeaning statements to women, such as "It's a tough world out there, honey, and you better catch up," as a means of intimidation. These are likely the same men who will make intimidating statements to other groups, saying for example, "When you get a little more experience out here, son, you'll learn this is the way we do it."

On the issue of whether women behave differently in a negotiation, Williams points out that in hundreds of studies on the issue, the evidence is split equally between women behaving differently, and women not behaving differently. Among those studies that indicate women behave differently, researchers came to the conclusion that females tend to be more cooperative than males. These same researchers have found that woman tend to be initially more trusting. Other researchers have also found that woman sit closer and generally show more cooperative nonverbal communication. Consistent with these findings is a study that shows that the more women act like stereotypical males, the more credibility they will have with men. Again, however, just as many studies indicate there is no difference.

---

14. Gerald R. Williams, A Lawyer's Handbook for Effective Negotiation and Settlement (1981).

CHAPTER 4
PREPARING AND PLANNING
FOR THE NEGOTIATION
INVOLVING THE CLIENT

A. In General

Adequately preparing and planning for the negotiation are crucial to success. However, lawyers frequently fail to give this adequate attention because of competing demands for their time. Good negotiating practice requires that you take whatever time is available to prepare for the negotiation, even if it is only ten minutes between meetings, or ten seconds as you leave your office to talk to a disgruntled staff member.

Obviously the more time you have, the more you can prepare. Because of discovery, you will frequently have access to a vast array of information about the parties, the events, and the alleged damages well before the face-to-face negotiation begins. In other circumstances you may not even know the name of the person with whom you are negotiating before he or she walks in the office door, such as a prosecutor in a large metropolitan area prosecuting 80 shoplifters a day. Even under this latter set of circumstances, you can effectively prepare if you are aware of the stages that must be completed in all negotiations.

Three broad issues must be dealt with in preparation and planning. First, you must identify what your client seeks to accomplish from the negotiation and what options are available to you to reach those goals. The adversarial negotiator converts those options into a position which he or she seeks to convince the other side to accept. For example, the client identifies, with his lawyer's help, the goal of having an income stream to allow the client to live comfortably despite permanent injuries received in an automobile accident. An infinite number of alternative positions ranging from zero to billions of dollars exist on the issue of enough money. The adversarial negotiator working with the client identifies the least advantageous alternative along this continuum that the client is willing to accept (e.g., the least he or she will accept). We typically call this the negotiator's bottom line or walk away price. The adversarial negotiator will then identify an opening position along this continuum as an opening offer or demand.

A problem-solver is less likely to stake out either a bottom line or an opening position, but must still identify the client's goals and any potential solutions that will allow these goals to be achieved. For example, a problem-solving lawyer, having identified an income stream as the goal, is likely to see a set amount of money in settlement as merely one possible solution. If providing a certain quality of life is the real goal, lump-sum payments are only one way to meet that goal. Other possibilities are structured settlements or the possibility of money plus training. Rather than immediately focusing on a limited number of positions, the problem-solver will begin thinking of numerous alternative ways to achieve the goal.

The second broad issue that you must address in preparation and planning concerns analyzing information to determine what you believe to be the other side's goals and any perceived solutions to meet those goals. The adversarial negotiator asks herself what is the likely position the other side will take, and what is their probable bottom line. The problem-solver begins to ask what the other side likely wishes to achieve and what they will likely see as appropriate ways to achieve that goal. To accomplish this task, both types of negotiators must begin assessing the information presently available to them and begin thinking about the additional information they would like to have. To the extent this information is available from sources other than the person with whom you are negotiating, preparation requires obtaining this information.

The third broad task in preparation and planning is to begin deciding how you are going to achieve your goals in the negotiation. The list of decisions can be quite long. The overriding question, however, is quite simple: How can you maximize your success in this negotiation?

If you accept this book's premise—that a systematic approach based on a multi-stage process will allow you to achieve better results—the question then is, what do I do to make my approach effective? At this point we have a bit of a chicken and egg problem because we have not fully identified the stages. It will come as no surprise given the above discussion, that gathering information will be critical. We must ask, therefore, what steps do we take to maximize acquiring information?

B. Determining Your Client's Needs, Interests, and Desires—The Necessity of Effective Client Counseling

Effective client counseling is critical to effective negotiation. For the adversarial negotiator to determine a bottom line or for the problem-solver to assess needs and to begin developing alternative solutions to the problem being negotiated presupposes (1) that the client has effectively articulated those goals, and (2) with your help the client has begun to identify acceptable solutions.

Pre-negotiation counseling typically focuses on a process that moves the client toward at least tentative decisions. Whether those decisions relate to the potential terms of a settlement in a personal injury lawsuit or the ultimate structure of a business arrangement in a transactional negotiation, you must have the client work through at least an elementary decision-making model.

Although there are certainly more sophisticated, or at least more complex, decision-making models, for our purposes a relatively simple model will suffice. Whether intuitively or systematically, what we typically do in working with clients who need to make a decision is to first identify their goal. What do they want to get out of the negotiation? Quite often the client has multiple goals and he will need to decide which are critical and which he can live without. In *Newman v. Popcheck*, for example, the plaintiff may have the goals of returning to the firm as a launch pad for a new job, of getting back pay and bonuses, and of punishing the firm. If you represent the plaintiff, you must have Ms. Newman prioritize these goals. She must consider whether the goals are mutually exclusive.

In helping the client identify the goals they seek to achieve, you must be careful to distinguish their goals from their position in the negotiation. Goals tend to be broader aspirations. For example, Ms. Newman may say her goal is to make Popcheck, et al pay her a great deal of money. While this may indeed be a goal, it may also be only a reflection of a position designed to achieve a different, perhaps broader result. After careful discussion you may find that what Ms. Newman really wants is for Popcheck and the firm to admit their behavior and be punished in a way that minimizes the likelihood the behavior will occur again. Newman's desire for a large amount of money is merely one way of achieving the broader goal.

After goals have been clarified, you must next help the client identify possible solutions to achieve those goals. The range of possible solutions available to Ms. Newman are somewhat limited if the goal is to achieve a large cash settlement. She may have considerably more alternatives if punishment is the goal.

As just stated, after you have identified the broad goal, you next begin identifying options which will allow you to meet those goals. If you focus on a cash settlement, you can identify an infinite number of options ranging from zero to billions of dollars. Each of these options will then be viewed in terms of positive and negative consequences.

Certainly one of the most significant types of consequences you can weigh will be the economic consequence of an alternative. Again, take the simple personal injury settlement example where the only issue is dollar amount. You and your client will consider the positive economic consequences of seeking a large settlement: acquiring a large amount of money that will make life comfortable for as long as the client lives. The negative economic consequence of seeking that large settlement may be that first, the demand is unlikely to be successful and second, opposing counsel may not take your position seriously, causing the negotiations to fail before they even get started.

More than economic consequences, however, will be considered. Remember our discussion of the social and psychological dynamic in the negotiation in Chapter 3. These social and psychological pressures affect our decision-making. Therefore, whether intuitively or systematically, you will factor social and psychological consequences into your assessment of the relative merits of options. A positive psychological benefit in seeking the large settlement might be that the client will feel that he or she is finally on the offense, standing tall, and "Not taking it any more." A negative psychological consequence may be that given the unlikely acceptance by the other side, your client will continue to worry about the lawsuit and its related effects on his or her life. If a client is being pushed by a spouse, a positive social benefit of the alternative will be that the spouse is not angry with the client's position. On the other hand, a negative social consequence may be that a spouse may be angered by the excessive demand.

Balancing all the consequences—both positive and negative—you and the client will conclude that at some dollar amount, the negatives outweigh the positives. If you adopt an adversarial approach, your search for a bottom line or walk away position ends when you find this point. In our example, it may be that the positive consequences of accepting $50,000 outweigh the negatives. At $49,999.99 the negatives may outweigh the positives and, therefore, be unacceptable.

The types of consequences affecting a particular negotiation will vary with the circumstances being negotiated. The economic consequences of a particular settlement will vary greatly. You can, however, identify a number of general categories. First is the direct economic payoff of the particular deal. Will the client be financially better off as a result of this agreement? If you are representing a company in the sale of a major asset, your client will consider such items as the cost of production, value of goods, how much the market will bear, desire to cultivate a relationship with the purchaser, availability of other suppliers, storage costs, and alternate dispositions of the asset.

You may also consider collateral economic factors, such as the cost of agreeing or not agreeing to the sale, or whether the result of this deal will affect your ability to get other deals. If you do agree to a certain economic solution, consider whether the result, if it becomes general knowledge, will cause the next person you negotiate with to expect the same treatment? How about lost work? Will the cost of getting a particular deal take more time than it is worth?

The social and psychological consequences also will vary from deal to deal, but there are some common types of social relationships that you should consider. Not surprisingly, these are similar to those discussed in Chapter 3. For example, if you have to deal with a person on a social level, it is possible it might impact your decision.

This process is as critical to an adversarial negotiator as it is to a problem-solving negotiator. While the problem-solver may not convert options into positions (over which debate proceeds during the negotiation) clarifying goals, identifying alternatives, and understanding various consequences are essential for you to develop creative problem-solving solutions.

In a particular negotiation, of course, your options may be more varied than accepting or rejecting a fungible item like money. Indeed, a problem-solver is likely to only tentatively fill out such a chart, because the problem-solver would expect that as the parties discuss the underlying needs, interests, and desires, they will identify additional options. Still, you may find it useful to begin clarifying the advantages and disadvantages of known options by listing them like the example on the next page for the plaintiff in *Newman v. Popcheck and Popcheck, Blink & Denis.*

Newman—Goals and Options	
Goals:	Be compensated for economic loss caused by termination and punish firm so that it will not happen again.
Option 1:	Rehire Newman with credit toward partnership of time since termination, payment of back wages during time of termination, and apology for termination.
Advantages:	Economic damages covered. Apology acts as punishment
Disadvantages:	No guarantee that Newman won't be fired in the future or that partnership share will not be adversely affected. Apology is private and no guarantee that corrective action will be taken. It will be an unpleasant place to spend professional career.
Option 2:	Payment of lost wages from date of termination until new employment is found and payment of $100,000 in punitive damages.
Advantages:	Continued receipt of money to carry on search for new meaningful employment. $100,000 will make significant economic impact on firm to encourage corrective action, while at the same time making client feel good about the result because of clear vindication.
Disadvantages:	Lost "equity" in credit toward partnership at a prestigious law firm. Vindication is essentially private and money does not guarantee corrective action.

Of course, the foregoing is just the tip of the iceberg. In a complex "bet the company" case the lawyer must think strategically regarding furthering the client's goals and implementing the client's objectives on a wide range of issues. It requires that the lawyer not only understand the "end game" if other dispute resolution processes fail, but it means the lawyer must understand different dispute resolution methods and the strengths and weaknesses of each. For example, lawyers must understand not only negotiation strategy, the ins and outs of mediation, and the pitfalls of arbitration, but also bankruptcy law, intellectual property law, antitrust law, and the companion procedural laws regarding removal, joinder, interpleader, multidistrict litigation, and class actions. Regardless of the process and substantive law setting in which the lawyer works, the lawyer must always see the process as a means to the client's objectives, and be willing to consider switching, when possible, from one process and setting to another if another process might work better to serve the client's goals. Key, then, is to inform, advise, and involve the client in a choice of dispute resolution processes. Their understanding of these choices will be vital to the implementation of their goals, as they will often be active players at various stages of each process.

Negotiation theory and practice, and the complementary field of conflict resolution, lay at the heart of each of these frameworks for dispute resolution. They are keys to a lawyer's understanding the strategies involved in different dispute resolution processes and settings. This chapter will focus on negotiation and conflict resolution theory, as it informs lawyer/client strategy in every step of the litigation process.

Strategic Perspectives

At the heart of dispute resolution is the management of information; what you give to the other parties and what you get from the other side. Information is the key to the accurate evaluation of the dispute, and a vital element in the prediction of the likely outcome.[15] Understanding how information management affects outcomes, will help the litigator strategically plan for conflict resolution that will best serve the client's goals.

In some ways, then, the litigation process itself, (whether finally resolved by the parties, or with the help of a mediator or adjudicator) is one big negotiation/information exchange process. The litigation process is the default, and is itself designed so that the parties learn about

---

15 Gary Williams, LEGAL NEGOTIATION AND SETTLEMENT (1983); Bastrass & Harbaugh, INTERVIEWING, COUNSELING, AND NEGOTIATION (1990).

each other's facts, values, perspectives on law, predictions of outcome, and, if the parties do not resolve their dispute for themselves, the court learns about these same facts, values, perspectives on law, and predictions of outcomes, and reaches a decision. In litigation, each side discovers as best it can the other's view of the predicted value of the case in the eyes of the decision maker and if there is any overlap, the parties settle. It is a decision-making process that is based on economics, on rationality, and wealth maximization. Settlement is the outcome in more than ninety-five percent of cases so the process seems to work pretty well most times. Sometimes parties complain about the expense of getting themselves in a position to determine the value of the case. But, still, under the position bargaining model of negotiation, the process is designed to empower the parties to settle when they rationally should settle. Even where the parties resort to a court, the court's decision itself may not finally resolve the dispute, but instead provide the parties with further information and leverage to reach a different and even better settlement that better fits their needs.

It is important to recognize the values inherent in the adversary system. The traditional approach to litigation is premised on the model that better decisions are made if each side must test its information by evidence in front of an unbiased decision maker. This process is based on the model of a fight, or competitive game, rather than on the basis of a cooperative model bent on getting at the truth. Embedded in the adversarial process is a *position bargaining* model of dispute resolution. The parties both seek information that will allow them to value their cases, and hide information from the other side, of which the other side might take advantage. From the information they are able to discover, each party then determines whether there is any overlap between their positions, and seeks by threats and persuasion to move the other side closer and closer to its bottom line position, the position at which it would rather take a settlement than risk the uncertain outcome of a trial.

The parties do not provide information to each other freely. (Granted, the new FRCP tries to change this by requiring information exchanges. Still the risk of discovery is that the other side has not revealed everything, and so the court must test its evidence at trial.) They seek to only inform the other side about those facts that they must turn over because of discovery rules. The adversarial nature of the process is inherent in the rules that dictate what the parties' responsibilities are with regard to discovery. Information exchange in negotiation also seems to be driven by the assumption that you have uncertain information, at best, about your opponent's weaknesses, and if you settle out of court before putting people under oath at trial, you risk settling for too much. *Position bargaining* strategies best test what cards the other side actually holds. Your positions serve as bets in the gamble of litigation, and *may* inform each side on what cards each holds. Position bargainers use their positions to get information, and elicit a willingness to settle. While this exchange often occurs on the courthouse steps, it might also occur after jury selection, opening statements, after the jury has started to deliberate, or even on appeal.

A classic example of position bargaining occurs in a bazaar or market place. Imagine you are at an open air market in Beijing. You stop at a table and pick up a shirt. The vendor says, "Do you like? For you, special price. One hundred yuan." You say, "Too much." The vendor says, "How much?" You say, "Thirty yuan." The vendor says, "No, how about two shirts for one hundred and fifty yuan." You say, "No, the most I pay is fifty yuan." They say no. You start to walk a way. They say, "Fine," and throw the shirt at you. You pay fifty yuan.

Position bargainers use positions to get information about what the other side really thinks. They posture and bluff to try to force movement. They provide little information about why or how they determine the price. We don't know what the buyer wants the shirt for, or how much the seller has in mark up or carrying costs. Reasons are not given. The parties think of the exchange as purely voluntary. Each may use psychology, and threats, and try to raise the sunk costs of each side by dragging out the time of bargaining. They may use the pressure of the public audience to shame the other into moving. But in the end, the process is governed by getting information by taking positions, to test what each side thinks the transaction is worth.

C. Position Bargaining

1. An Analytical Economic Model

Assume, for a minute, however, that each side had perfect information about the other side's case. Assume that discovery has been completed and each side has all that it can legally expect to get. Position bargainers still must predict the outcome at trial as a way of determining the fair price of resolving the dispute. Every lawyer knows the dangers of prediction. Predicting victory can raise false expectations in the client, making the client spend the money before the client gets it.

It also subjects the lawyer to the, "But you said..." from the client, when the prediction doesn't come true. Still the client is entitled to make an informed decision when giving the lawyer settlement authority for negotiation purposes. And the question is whether economic models which use probabilities will provide the useful language of prediction in order for the client to make informed decisions. In fact, the question of whether to use probabilities may be moot, because clients seem to be demanding as much. Certainly business clients and/or client insurers want a probability of success in order to set up reserves. And consumers demand it of their doctors, so why not of their lawyers?

In order to use economics and probabilities to provide the client with information about what their case is worth, the lawyer first needs to be clear about what economic modeling and probabilities really provide. The beauty of economic analysis is that for every real world problem that makes prediction impossible, you simply make an assumption. And the result is a "mathematic-like" formula that gives the appearance of a scientific method, or certainty, and of objectivity. Perhaps it gives a false impression. In addition, a second dangerous assumption the economist makes is that jurors are rational. They also assume perfect information about a case will be produced by the litigation process and trial. The question is whether these assumptions are so false and will so cloud any probabilities that the probabilities will become misleading rather that helpful.

On the other hand, the lawyer needs to start someplace in communicating his legal assessment of the case, and with these two assumptions in mind, the lawyer can start to predict how jurors will likely calculate damages in a given case. Let's give it a try...for *analytically and strategically speaking*, we might be able to create a formula that will make us more precise in valuing our case and better able to inform the client about what to expect. The corollary benefits are also substantial. A by-product of making an economic calculation for cases in order to place a value on the case provides more information to the client so that the client can truly control the outcome. A second by-product of using economic tools will be to give the lawyers more persuasive arguments in their negotiations about what the case is worth, and provide the language to move their opponents off their position (provided our reasoning doesn't open up counter arguments to our disadvantage).

As we have said, before actually communicating with the client, the lawyer should look at the case from the perspective of the jury, or the end game perspective. First, in a typical tort situation (assuming the jury has perfect information, as presented through the trial process), the jury will need to determine the percentage of fault of each party. It then adds up the fault attributed to the defendants (depending on joint and several liability rules), and subtracts the amount of fault attributed to the plaintiff to come up with percentages of liability. Of course, in a jurisdiction that is not a "pure comparative" jurisdiction, this works. Juries figuring close cases in "fifty-percent jurisdictions," (where the plaintiff is barred from recovery where the plaintiff's fault is equal to or greater than the defendants), may lean toward the plaintiff to make sure the plaintiff gets something—at least if they know about the results of finding forty-nine or fifty percent liability on the part of the plaintiff. Some jurisdictions don't tell the jury.

Second, if the jury determines there is compensable liability, then the jury needs to figure damages. Damages are made up of "hard damages" like 1) past medical expenses in personal injury cases and 2) past lost income figures (loss of business from product disparagement) and then "softer damages," including 1) predictions on future medical expenses, and 2) future loss of income, and finally "softest damages," for 1) pain and suffering, or 2) humiliation and mental anguish, or 3) loss of consortium, or 4) loss of "hedonic" damages (e.g. the pleasure of playing the piano) or, 5) loss to future trade, and/ or 6) punitive damages, to send a message to the defendant and like defendants to deter future behavior.

Third, the jury will need to multiply the percentage of fault by the total amount of damages found. Or, depending on joint and several liability rules, it simply takes the total damages and subtracts the percentage of fault attributed to the plaintiff to come up with a figure for damages.

Yet in predicting what the jury will actually do in such a case, the lawyer knows that there are a lot of "nonrational" factors that the jury may take into account. The particular judge may exercise a lot of subtle control over the process. Marginally relevant good or bad facts may significantly affect the outcome (like evidence that one of the parties is a saint, or that one is not a nice person). The jury may consciously or subconsciously take race into account, or age, or sex, or may be biased against corporations, or angry at institutions and governments who make their lives difficult, especially where injury occurs to protected classes like the elderly, pregnant women, or children. The lawyer on the other side may be a particularly wonderful communicator, having demonstrated talent in bringing in spectacular verdicts for her clients. Finally, the make-up of the jury needs to be considered, as jury verdicts of city/minority jurors tend to give more to some plaintiffs and rural or suburban jurors and upper/middle class jurors may give less. Selecting potential jurors from driver license registration versus voter registration can even make a large difference.

To try and factor these biases into any economic calculation, lawyers may try to determine a multiplier—that amount by which they multiply the "hard" economic damages in the case—to come up with a prediction as to what the jury will do. (These multipliers may be less relevant in commercial litigation where the sympathy factors or the communities' views have less effect when the dispute is between two parties that can take care of themselves. Or maybe they still do play a role, especially depending on the good will that company may have built up because of its community involvement and corporate image.) And so certain jurisdictions try to keep tabs on how much juries give in relation to the "hard" damages in the case. Historically Philadelphia or New York may have a multiplier of 4.5 to 5. Chesterfield, Virginia may have a multiplier of 2 to 3. Of, course any given case can and should be distinguished from the average verdicts, (just as with any jury verdict service)—arguing even about what are hard damages. And there are definitional problems with multipliers: for example, should future lost income be counted as hard damages in a particular case, or, should pain and suffering be greater or lesser when death was imminent. Still the multiplier can be a way of predicting how much over the hard damages the jury might pay in a given jurisdiction.

So, in a given case, a lawyer might value a personal injury case as follows:

$30,000 hospital
$60,000 future hospital (dis)*
$50,000 lost wages (+ int)
$500,000 future lost wages (dis)*

Total Special Damages	$640,000
Multiplier 4.5 =	**$2,880,000**

The difference is presumably made up in pain and suffering, emotional distress, and the like.

Further, the attorney needs to predict percentage of liability to plaintiff, say 30%.

30% of $2,880,000 =	$864,000
Net Damages	**$2,016,000**

Now, assuming that the probability figure is accurate, $2,016,000 is the lawyer's prediction of the most likely jury damages award.

Or, take, for instance, a client in a case who wants to seek a preliminary injunction against product disparagement. Here the prediction is about what the judge will likely do. The client may show a fall off in business in the past three months that they attribute to the alleged disparagement. They might project that if this disparagement continues, it could put them out of business. Assuming that they can show an income statement that shows net profits at $10 million a year, the losses they may show would amount to approximately $100 million over ten years. The chances that they might get an injunction might be five percent, but, they might be willing to spend $500,000 in litigation costs even if it is only a five percent chance of winning.

In a jury case, some attorneys also find it helpful knowing the latest percentages of plaintiff success once a case goes to a jury. For example, recent plaintiffs' lawyers quote a 70% win rate in front of Los Angeles County juries. Medical malpractice defense lawyers quote recent Center-for-State Courts statistics showing that doctors who are sued for malpractice win close to 60% of the time when the case goes to jury. (In fact, the center's statistics seemed to indicate that plaintiffs have a better chance to win if they try their case before only a judge.) These percentages can again add information to a lawyer's case evaluation, so long as the lawyer realizes the predictive nature of these figures and still assesses the biasing factors of the individual case.

In a judge decided case, a particular judge may be known by his or her track record to never give an injunction, and this may be useful in framing the prediction for the client.

Defendants' lawyers like to argue in negotiation that, economically speaking, the rational thing to do is weight each decision the jury needs to make by its probability of occurring in plaintiff's favor. So weighing duty, and weighing breach, proximate cause, and some damages, would mathematically result in a better understanding of the probabilities involved. Instead of giving a probability to the chances of winning, they give a probability to each element of the cause of action, and multiply them together. For example, if proving a duty existed was .9, breach was .5, proximate cause was .7, and proving some damage was .9, then the probability of plaintiff success would be .2835.

Similarly, the chance of getting a preliminary injunction needs to be viewed in light of the court deciding Popcheck's way on four different factors: the likelihood of success on the merits, the balance of harms, the adequate remedy at law, and on public policy issues (competition in the marketplace v. fair competition).

Yet probability weighting could be more sophisticated, but less complicated. In the garden variety personal injury case, the plaintiff might argue that if breach is proven, then proximate cause and damages are virtual certainties. In the personal injury example above, the probability might be .45 (duty multiplied by breach). Plaintiffs would cite to attitudinal studies which seem to indicate that accountability for ones behavior is the number one value in the United States today (according to *Time Magazine* Poll, Spring, 2000). The thinking would be that the jury would focus in on one tough decision concerning who is responsible—the blameworthiness of the defendant—and then simply do what was required after they made that decision.

There is some support for plaintiffs' arguments in Donald E. Vinson's book, *Jury Trials, The Psychology of Winning Strategy*, pp. 1–46, that jurors think deductively from certain strongly held values. This would mean that giving a single probability on liability may be a more accurate predictor. For the purpose of early case evaluation, then, focus groups may provide a quick and the most accurate prediction of what attitudes the jurors may have that are outcome determinative, and as a result best help the lawyer and client assess the case's chance of success before a jury. To create a focus group, pay $15 an hour to 12 persons whom you assemble that meet the demographics of your jury. Present opening statements on both sides, and for under $1,000 you can see where the jury is likely to come out. Of course, when the focus group has questions, and discovery and proof can be obtained, you might refine your theories and themes in the process. In any event, for purposes of telling the client what the case is worth, the focus group could be a good predictor of how the jury might respond to your case. Of course, the credibility of the witness will not be tested, but attitudinal values of the likely jurors could be surveyed to determine what the likely result would be.

Similarly, current thinking about preliminary injunctions suggests that balance of harms is a heavily weighted factor in determining whether a preliminary injunction should be issued. Lawyer-conducted probability analysis in injunction cases that under weighted this factor would not provide the client with an accurate understanding of whether the client should seek an injunction.

In addition, early involvement of damages experts is important for case evaluation. Used as a consulting expert, as opposed to a testifying expert, such consultants can provide invaluable information for the client's valuation of the case and decision making.

Moreover, the parties may use focus group results to help the parties value their cases. Just as focus groups test markets and their reactions to products and the marketing of products, so focus groups can provide clients with better empirical evidence of what their case may be worth. If fairly and objectively presented, then focus groups not only can give the parties insight into how to market their case, and what themes will best resonate with jurors, but they can help the sides persuade each other that groups of likely jurors will place high or low values on an "objective" presentation of the case.

Finally, for the purpose of developing settlement authority from the client, there are three additional economic forces that need to be calculated: 1) the expense already incurred and the expense involved in further trial preparation, 2) the expense of the trial itself, and 3) a discount factor till trial. (I'm assuming you have already figured in the discount rate for determining the present value of future income streams. Of course, if your jurisdiction doesn't discount because it reasons that inflation and discount balance out, then don't discount.) Dealing with number 3 first, in some jurisdictions, trial could still be a long way off, though if discovery is completed, as in the typical case, this is not likely a big factor. On the other hand if payment is going to be made over a significant period of time, as with structure payments, then counsel needs to be familiar with the present-value-of-money calculations to advise the client about settlement authority.

In sum, an economic value of a case for developing client settlement authority would include total damages, subtraction of plaintiff fault, a weighing of this figure on percentage chance of winning and proving damages as predicted, any discounting for present value, and costs yet to be incurred in producing the result, and/or subtraction of lawyer's contingency fees or lawyers fees.

PDL (probability of defendant held liable) x TD (total expected damages) x P (probability of damages finding) – PPCN (probability of plaintiff's contributory negligence) – PPND (probability of plaintiff's damages associated with plaintiff's negligence) – D (discount to present value) – C (costs) – LF (lawyer fee) = Case Value

Using this formula can help prepare the lawyer for meetings with the client to discuss the legal and economic consequences of a decision will help the lawyer be more precise in informing the client and to develop settlement authority. It will also help prepare the lawyer to be more persuasive during settlement negotiations.

2. Client Role in Position Bargaining

In this regard, we must turn to how the lawyer communicates this economic evaluation to the client. Of course, here is where the lawyer must be careful. In counseling the client, the plaintiff should be told how this figure depends on persuading the jury or decision maker about a number of key elements of the case, including duty, breach, proximate cause and damages. For example, the plaintiff needs to be told that the jury may see future hospital bills as potentially curing the ailment, or that the chances of the jury attributing thirty percent to the plaintiff depends on the court excluding evidence of plaintiff's drinking, because the Breathalyzer was under the legal limit. If this fails, the lawyer will wish to keep people who are religiously opposed to drinking off the jury.

An additional tip we'd like to pass on for communicating with clients is that some lawyers like to summarize all the variables of prediction by giving a percentage chance of winning and include giving a best possible alternative, a most likely alternative, a likely alternative, and a worst possible alternative. In our example above, the lawyer might then add two figures, in addition to the $2,880,000 best possible $2,016,000 most likely, and say $100,000 as a likely alternative, as the figure that covers the plaintiff's out of pocket, and that may give something to cover plaintiff's attorney's fees, and $0 as the worst alternative. The plaintiff might even weight these outcomes by percentage.

Best possible	20%	$2,880,000
Most likely	50%	$2,016,000
Likely	30%	$100,000
Worst possible	20%	$0

In any event, the client is armed with substantially better information to make an informed decision, and the negotiator is more precise about what he thinks the case is worth and why. *(Use display technology to teach the client your value of the case, and to help them understand your theme, and the opposing sides views of the case. See Chapter 5.)*

Moreover, the position bargainers argue that this kind of strategic thinking makes each side's thinking more objective and analytical. It better helps the bargainer control their own behavior during the negotiation, knowing the limits of their authority, and the steps they plan to take to arrive within a reasonable bottom line. In fact, each side's figures should not be that far apart. Often, experienced dispassionate business litigators prepare a valuation from the perspective of the opponent. Preparing from the opposing side's perspective better prepares the lawyer to anticipate the points of difference and prepare arguments to overcome those differences. This preparation process makes them better able to talk with each other and discover the strengths and weaknesses in each other's positions and reach a reasoned agreement. It is often the case that the lawyers work something out, even if on the courthouse steps, after jury *voir dire*, after opening statement, or after closing argument and before the jury reaches a verdict. Or, the clients work something out in spite of their lawyers' failures to communicate. When this happens, the clients are guessing about outcomes, and assessing risks in the light of their views of their business objectives.

Recognize, however, that the rationality of the probability assigning process depends on the quality of the information each side has. Moreover, the assignment of probabilities is an inherently value-laden process. Probabilities depend on experience, but experience is always seen through human eyes. So, where a CEO experiences law suits by the government, with eyes that see the market as having been harmed by excessive government regulation, the CEO may place a probability figure on the chances of a win, based on the CEO's chances at doing something about a broader societal issue. Or the plaintiff (and/or attorney) may demonize the opponent and place probabilities on the outcome at court based on these biasing beliefs. Building in a range of probabilities can at times still provide an analytical basis for reasoned agreement.

Yet the position bargainer knows that they must plan to conduct the negotiation itself in order to control the risks in any analytical approach to case valuation. They must test other side's case to determine how good its information is, and whether the values and perceptions of the opposing side so affect the valuation of the case, that their client is risking an unfair, disadvantageous resolution. The position bargainer sets up the negotiation, to help maximize its advantages concerning information exchange, bargaining positions, and persuasion to move the opposition toward its view of the value of the case.

D. Planning for Position Bargaining

In light of the foregoing discussion, consider how the strategic thinker would plan his litigation for a negotiated settlement using strictly a position bargaining approach.

1. Information Exchange

The first step is to determine what style and strategies are most likely to produce the most information without revealing your own. Is it best to be friendly, creating a cooperative competition for information, or is it better to be aggressively adversarial, and control and test information? Your thinking on this issue will help you plan out whether and how to select the forum, conduct icebreaking, assert agenda control, employ appropriate questioning strategies, and prepare blocks that will help maximize an information exchange that will provide access to how the opposing side values their case, the opposing side's weaknesses, and any emotional or psychological factors that may affect case valuation.

2. Response to Opening Offer

The negotiator needs to be careful not to "leak" too much information, non-verbally, when the opponent makes an offer. If they unintentionally reveal interest and acceptance, just like in a game of poker, they tip off the other side to what cards they hold.

3. Opening Offer

Prepare an opening offer that balances your credibility as a speaker with your position bargaining strategy of testing the other side's view of their and your case.

4. Persuasive Statements in Support of Your Positions

Prepare a detailed, multifaceted, appropriately passionate presentation in support of your offer. (*Use display technology!*)

Have it build one argument on top of another, and prepare to deliver it with the right emotional fervor.

5. Plan Your Concessions

Prepare ahead of time the timing of, size of, and decision factors that will give rise to concessions. The key is to prepare the size of the concession, because it can send signals as to where you have set the bottom line. Make sure to accompany each concession with a reason for your concession. Don't concede twice without your opponent conceding in between. (Do not bargain against yourself.) Note that you can initiate a second concession with a prior condition on the part of your opponent.

6. Test Your Opponent's Bottom Line

Know the ethical parameters of persuasion in the context of negotiations. Much has been written about the ethical issues in negotiation concerning the discussion of the client's bottom line. Recognize that if you ask your opponent, "Do you have authority to move off your last position?" you are putting them in a professional and tactical dilemma. If they have room to move, and say no, they risk deadlock, and are in a conflict with the authority their client has given them. On the other hand, giving up client confidences about the client's communications to the lawyer about his or her bottom line is unethical.

Ethical Parameters and Bottom Lines

Some have argued that negotiators are free to lie if they are asked about their client's willingness to settle. Model Rule 3.4 and Comment 2 to Model Rule 4.1 seem to indicate as much. Take a close look at Model Rules 3.4, 4.1, and comment 2 to 4.1.

> **MR 3.4 Fairness to Opposing Party and Counsel**
>
> —A lawyer shall not: falsify evidence, counsel or assist a witness to testify falsely, or offer an inducement to a witness that is prohibited by law.

MR 4.1 Truthfulness in Statements to Others

—In the course of representing a client a lawyer shall not knowingly

a) make a false statement of material fact or law to a third person; or

b) fail to disclose a material fact to a person when disclosure is necessary to avoid assisting in a criminal or fraudulent act by a client, unless disclosure is prohibited by Rule 1.6.

Comment 2. Statements of Fact

—[2] ...Whether a particular statement should be regarded as one of fact can **depend on the circumstances**. Under the generally accepted conventions in negotiation, certain types of statements ordinarily are not taken as statements of material fact. **Estimates of price or value** placed on the subject of a transaction and a party's **intentions as to an acceptable settlement** of a claim are in this category,...

When you ask about your opponent's bottom line, or when they ask you about yours, you have created, or are facing, a dilemma. If you say you do not have authority to move, you may lock yourself in at the expense of settlement. Consider each of the following options:

- ❖ Based on what you have told me so far, I can't recommend that my client move off the earlier position.

- ❖ You first! Can you move any more off of your earlier position?

❖   I've been given broad discretion by my client, but I'm not willing to move, based on what I've learned so far.

Others try to manipulate the client's "bottom line" during a negotiation. They may counsel their client to give them only limited authority during the early stages of negotiation, so that they can use their client to slow down the bargaining process and get client input as more is learned about the other side's position.

7. Prepare for Deadlock

One of the problems with deadlock is that you must take the steps to prepare for trial, knowing that there might be other grounds of fruitful discussion that may lead to the resolution of the dispute. You should plan how to deal will deadlock. Will you walk out? Will you stay and bargaining hypothetically? This way you might be able to brainstorm with your opponent for creative ways to deal with the deadlock. You might take the opportunity presented by the deadlock to bargain like problem-solvers (see discussion below.)

8. Wrap up

Prepare to restate the terms of the agreement to be clear that you have a deal on each issue that is important to your client.

9. Write up

Plan ahead of time for who will write up the deal. Save some emotional energy for the write up. Parties can add or try to subtract from what has been agreed to during the write up stage. Be careful here not to celebrate too early, leaving yourself no reservoir of energy, in case there are still problems with the deal.

E. Anticipate Other Side's Bargaining Range

Having identified your client's goals, you must next assess the other side's probable position. Here, as in other parts of the negotiation process, it is useful to place yourself in the position of the other side. If you have gone through a decision-making process described in the previous section, it is possible the other side has as well. As such, you should assess the available information to judge the likely goals the other side may have, as well as the options they are likely to have identified as meeting these goals. You then should start assessing the information available to you to determine the consequences that are perceived by the other side. What information do you have available to you to determine the likely positive and negative economic, social, and psychological consequences?

Having assessed the available information, the next logical step is to determine what additional information you need and how you can get access to the information. A lot of information is, of course, available through formal and informal discovery. Where information is obtainable only from the other side, you must decide how best to acquire that information. For a discussion of acquiring this type of information see Chapter 6 on Information Bargaining.

An adversarial negotiator will find it useful to view the process of determining the other side's bottom line in light of our adversarial versus problem-solving approaches of negotiation. Take for example, the situation described in *Newman v. Popcheck and Popcheck, Blink & Denis*. The following diagram illustrates the plaintiff's negotiation plan:

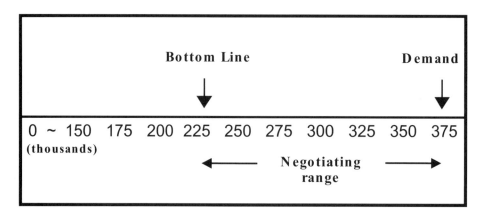

The next step for an adversarial negotiator is to begin gathering and assessing information to recreate the other side's bargaining range. In a perfect world, with perfect information and an idiot on the other side, adversarial negotiation is a process by which you seek information sufficient to judge the other side's bottom line and then offer it to them. Of course, in the real world there is not perfect information, and all other people are not idiots. In our example, you might assume that the opening position of the other side is that no payment will be made. What you are trying to assess is information that will let you decide how far up the scale the person is willing to go. Because you made your decision based on economic, social, and psychological consequences and their relative importance to you, as an adversarial negotiator, you must seek the same type of information from the other side that will allow you to recreate their decision-making. Graphically, it might be presented as follows:

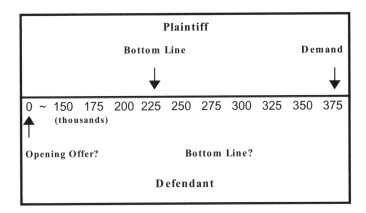

The problem-solver is going to seek and assess the same type of information. Rather than seeking the information to fathom a bottom line, the problem-solver wants the information so that he or she can determine the needs, interests, and desires that have to be met. If the problem-solver can identify these needs, interests, and desires (economic, social, and psychological considerations) he can then begin considering and proposing alternative solutions which will satisfy both sides.

A problem-solver will also seek to develop alternative perceptions of the problem in such a way that additional proposals can be created. In *Newman*, for example, the problem-solver will recognize that plaintiff's demand for $450,000 is merely their proposed solution to what plaintiff sees as an underlying problem. The problem-solver will try to determine the needs, interests, and desires that underlie the position and attempt to jointly formulate a solution that meets those needs, interests, and desires. The problem-solver in proposing a solution may well end up rejecting a narrow definition of the issue as how much money will be paid, and reformulate the issue to: "How do we ensure Ms. Newman's uninterrupted professional development?"

A problem-solver will use this approach in a wide variety of circumstances. Assume you are negotiating with a bank on behalf of a business client who is trying to avoid bankruptcy. The bank, quite predictably, may have expressed increasing discomfort with the loan. As a result of the bank's perceived (indeed very real) increased risk the bank seeks to increase the rate on a line of credit. The adversarial negotiator from the bank will determine the level of risk the bank faces, and equating rate with level of risk, determine the minimum rate acceptable to cover the risk while simultaneously trying to determine the maximum rate the customer is likely to pay. The problem-solving lawyer might try to recharacterize the negotiation and seek information about the bank's underlying concerns while trying to explain past failures on the part of the client.

This may result in finding that the underlying business is quite good, but that the customer is unable to exercise competent fiscal management and has a lousy accounting system. The problem-solver might also find out that these are the bank's expertise. While the rate may go up, the problem-solver might be able to minimize the rate increase by agreeing to "purchase" services from the bank that work toward solving the underlying business problem.

F. Negotiation Strategy and Client Counseling

Formulating and implementing a problem-solving negotiation strategy is integrally connected to client counseling. If you have chosen a problem-solving approach you may have a challenging educational process on your hands regarding the client. To be the most effective problem-solver you need the client to buy into taking a more creative problem-solving approach to try to reach an early settlement. You will need a more detailed and complete understanding of the client's goals and values. The better the lawyer understands the client, the better the lawyer will be able to determine a value for the case, the bottom lines for both parties, and create strategies for building trust and relationships between the parties. But also, the better the lawyer understands the client's goals and values, the better the lawyer can search for a more particularized problem-solving solution.[16]

Still, in the real world of lawyer negotiation, despite the careful planning of the negotiator, the opposition may not want to play. It may use the apparent cooperative setting to block giving truthful information and discover the weaknesses in your case, without any trade of information and understanding of the weaknesses in its own case. Some even argue, that as in the international arena, it is ineffective if not unethical for a bargainer to worry about anything but his client's (nation's) own interests. Some assert that position-bargaining strategies are a matter of human nature (inherent selfishness): that human nature dictates behavior that requires the negotiator to be suspicious of and mistrust his opponents, and see any attempt to be open and cooperative as a ma-

---

16   Robert H. Mnookin, Beyond Winning, Chapter 7.

nipulative strategy designed to give his opponent undue leverage in the resolution of the dispute.

In any event, lawyers need to be cautious in implementing problem-solving models when their opponents may not be bargaining in good faith. It is important to realize, however, the advantages of cooperative problem-solving in order to advise the client about the potential use of a mediator. Moreover, the lawyer needs to understand these two different strategies and approaches to negotiation—both position bargaining and problem-solving, in order to plan and advise the client about the potential strategic uses of a mediator to help resolve the dispute. (See Chapter 9.)

G. Planning to Implement the Negotiation Process

Once you have assessed existing information concerning the other side's position, you must next address a third area of preparation and planning: What steps should be planned and taken to maximize the success of the systematic framework we are trying to implement? Any number of process issues exist. How will you set the agenda? How will you ask questions? When will you make your first offer? Other questions arise that relate to specific stages in the process. Let's look at a few of these issues.

1. Your Place or Theirs

Where should you conduct the negotiation? This question is instructive because it illustrates that a systematic approach may lead you to a conclusion that is contrary to popular wisdom. Many books on negotiation will tell you to always have the person come to your turf. It creates a psychological advantage for you; they have already made a concession and it puts you in the "power position." Such a rule is, however, inconsistent with the premise of this book—choice is critical.

You may get a psychological advantage by negotiating in your office. If you concentrate on the issue of information gathering, however, you will see that the answer is not so clear. Ask yourself, "If information is critical, where am I likely to get the most information, my office or theirs?" Looking at it simply as a question of where information is stored, you will likely get more information at their place. Viewing their surroundings will give you a great deal of information about the substance of the negotiation and the other side's personality. A lawyer's visit to a potential business partner will give that lawyer information about that person or business just from the physical surroundings.

If you want documentary information, going to opposing counsel's office may also make more sense, because he will have a harder time saying, "Gee, I don't have that with me," than if he were in your office. On perhaps a bit more sophisticated level, people are generally more comfortable on their own turf. As comfort goes up people are generally more willing to talk. Because the more they talk the more information you get, it once again may make sense to meet in their office.

You have to choose, given the particular negotiation, which place is better. In fact, you may decide a third location or the telephone is best. There may be considerations that lead you to negotiate by phone despite some of its obvious disadvantages, such as loss of nonverbal communication and access to other information. If, for example, you are intimidated by the other person, the telephone allows you to place distance between you and that person and to hide your own insecurity.

The above discussion assumes that you are able to control location. In certain circumstances your only choice will be between doing the negotiation at one location or not negotiating. When your boss calls, you will probably meet wherever the boss wants to meet. Similarly, telephone negotiation is often required because of practical considerations of time and distance. Your only choice is between using the telephone or not negotiating.

Of course, we have many considerations even with an issue as straightforward as where the negotiation is to take place. Information, although important, is not everything, and you must consider other factors. Among other factors that make negotiating at your place an advantage are:

❖ your ultimate authority source may be easier to contact;

❖ avoiding the inconvenience of being removed from other obligations;

❖ the psychological advantage that the other side came to you;

❖ saving money and travel time;

❖ managing atmosphere, including being able to control interruptions.

On the other hand, additional advantages of going to the other side's site include:

- ❖ concentrating fully on the interaction;
- ❖ the other side must deal with interruptions;
- ❖ easily leaving someone's office, rather than asking someone to leave yours;
- ❖ communicating a willingness to work with the individual by going to the trouble of visiting them.

2. Determining a Purpose/Developing an Agenda

How are you going to control the negotiation process? Beyond getting information, you need to ask how much information do you need and what kind of information do you seek? A particular meeting, for example, may simply be a get-acquainted meeting where the emphasis will be on developing a relationship. Acquiring information relevant to a particular agreement might be secondary. On the other hand, the meeting may be one in which you choose to seek as much information as possible about the other side so that you can prepare a detailed proposal to submit at a later time. What you expect to get should in part determine how you structure the negotiation session.

You can also plan how you are going to obtain the information. Are you going to use open-ended questions or narrow questions? Will you proceed to the point of asking for precise pieces of information, or will you stick to generalities at this stage?

3. Determining Personal Attributes to Take into the Negotiation

You can plan what your style is going to be during the negotiation. We change our personality quite often in unconscious ways. We act differently at home and at work. Our personality with a superior may be significantly different from our interaction with a co-worker. We make these changes consciously and we should to the extent that it fosters our goals. You can choose to be cooperative or adversarial depending on what you are seeking. You can be open about your feelings or closed. You can communicate a structured approach to interviewing or an unstructured approach. The possibilities are limitless. Here, as with all aspects of the interpersonal process, the idea is to choose to act in a certain manner for a specific purpose.

Related to personality traits is the idea that you are able to plan to play or not play certain roles. Society often defines certain roles for individuals and you should decide whether playing that role is to your advantage. We know that a lawyer with a large firm in a major metropolitan area may have a public perception quite different from a solo practitioner in a rural area. Whether these roles or stereotypes are accurate or not, you can decide whether to fit into that stereotype. A particular person you are negotiating with may react favorably to it, whereas a client may not.

4. Planning the Setting

The setting of the negotiation is often something that you can plan. We have already discussed location, but if the negotiation is going to take place at your location, you should think about the physical setting. As will be discussed in more detail in Chapter 6, nonverbal communication can impact the session. Furniture arrangement may facilitate or inhibit the exchange of information. Research suggests that people seek some barrier, but not too great a barrier between themselves and the person they are talking to.

A lawyer sitting behind a desk with the opposing lawyer sitting directly across may get less information than if the two sit around a low coffee table. Some psychologists would also say that the absence of any barrier can inhibit communication. The feeling that you are invading the "space" of the other person may increase their anxiety level to a point where it inhibits communication.

If resources permit, plan the setting to meet some happy medium and have sufficient flexibility to allow for differing personalities you may interview. The common setup of a sofa and chair at right angles allows the person to position herself at a comfortable distance from the other negotiator. Something as simple as having chairs with wheels may allow you the needed flexibility.

5. Choosing a Strategy

Another important planning question is whether you are going to be an adversarial negotiator, problem-solver, or some mix of the two? Will you be competitive, cooperative, or something in between? You should also begin to anticipate the other side's probable strategies. Are they likely to be adversarial negotiators or problem-solvers? You should develop intermediate positions short of your bottom line and be able to justify each of those positions. If you are willing to offer a prospective associate an annual salary of $45,000, would you prefer $40,000? If so, should you start by offering $35,000? Given what you know about this person, will offering less hurt the long-term relationship?

You should also investigate any controlling principles and determine whether they must or should be followed. Your ability to negotiate may be restricted by statutes, regulations, or rules of professional responsibility. Often you can question conventions that may apply. If you are selling a major asset, purchasers may expect you to set the price. A convention in most purchase and sale settings is that the seller sets the price. You might like to avoid doing this, at least early on, because price always depends on the other side's needs and you might want more time to assess these needs.

PROBLEM 4.1

Assume you are hiring a new staff member to work in your law office.

What conventions, or controlling principles, are there that you should be aware of?

How might you change these expected conventions?

In the above problem, a convention often at work in the employment setting is that, not surprisingly, the employer sets the salary. If you are hiring someone, you might want to reject this convention if you have insufficient information as to the appropriate salary. You may already do this intuitively if you have ever asked someone what their salary needs are. Prospective employers also commonly ask for a salary history before the interview takes place. Both of these actions are ways to change a controlling convention that an employer makes the first offer on salary.

6. Plan Use of Extra-Negotiation Factors

Plan the use of extra-negotiation factors. Can regulators, insurers, arbitrators, or mediators be helpful? For more details, see the discussion in Chapter 9 on alternate dispute resolution.

7. Everything Else

These implementation issues are examples of the many parts of a negotiation that you must plan. In the chapters that follow as we identify what we need to do to implement the negotiation, we will simultaneously identify additional areas that require preparation and planning. It may be obvious, but it is still worth saying: If you have to do something in a negotiation, you have to plan how you are going to do it. Thorough preparation requires you to go through each stage of the negotiation and ask what do I need to do, and how am I going to do it?

Planning for Adversarial Bargaining
• Carefully determine weaknesses of your own case and prepare blocking strategies
• Gather all the information on opponent's strengths and weaknesses and "sunk costs"
• Plan information exchange with pointed and insistent follow-up questions
• If blocked, plan to identify block as evidence of weakness and expressly assume the information in your favor
• Plan an opening offer that is high enough to risk little in the way of true assessment of your bottom line
• Plan a detailed persuasive statement that is multifaceted
• Plan a dismissive reaction to opponent's opening offer but probe it for leakage
• Plan small concessions to signal little room to move
• Plan to use time and deadlock to test opponent's real positions
• Plan to use threats, anger, and irrationality to force movement
• Enlist client if producing "false authority"

PTER 5

ISCUSSIONS:
SETTING THE AGENDA

y any interpersonal communication,
ss of ice breaking. This stage typically
eatening topics. Every good negotia-
e for this to take place. Ice breaking
s. Primarily, this stage focuses on de-
hip with the other side. Small talk at
places the other person more at ease,
s, the willingness to provide informa-

n opportunity for you, the lawyer, to
level may be higher than normal and
eatening topics it should help decrease

opportunity to gather information dur-
ou with a good opportunity to gather
side, view their personality traits, and
them. Also, ice breaking is a good op-
luate you. When you refer to a picture
rson with whom you are negotiating,
, she's a cute kid, but then that's not
ved important information about that
e to set up a pattern of interaction.

ary for ice breaking is a reflection of
mportant of these factors are: 1) prior
vailable time; and 3) the other person's
tionship the ice breaking at a particu-
n non-existent. This may merely be a
aking has been going on for years and
been met. A new relationship will nor-

mally require more time to allow both you and the other person to meet the goals.

Typically, people naturally fall into some type of ice breaking or small talk. Too often, however, ice breaking is ineffective in terms of our goals because it proceeds along the following lines:

LAWYER 1 (L1): Ms. Jones, thanks for coming in today. Did you have any trouble finding the office?

LAWYER 2 (L2): Oh, no, not at all.

L1: Good. I know parking can be kind of difficult around here, especially in the rain.

L2: Yes, I can't believe this weather.

L1: So, how can I help you?

Perhaps the biggest problem with this type of exchange is the topic. These topics are so obviously ice breaking that the participants never get beyond a stilted "obligatory" exchange that merely provides a transition to the important part of the negotiation. It is the equivalent of the statement, "How are you doing?" as you pass a colleague in the hall. Each knows the other is not at that time really interested in a response to the substance of the question.

To effectively meet our goals for ice breaking, the discussion must proceed more naturally, covering topics that do not invite a reaction that this is a mere formality. Having this type of discussion is obviously easier with someone with whom you already have an established relationship. The relationship gives you a common background of information which allows you to pick a topic you can feel comfortable with and that will be both non-threatening and interesting. A person who has a family can be asked, "How is John doing at college?"

The goal for situations without a preexisting relationship is to evaluate the information available, however limited, to see if you can find a non-threatening topic to discuss. When visiting a person's place of business this is much easier because your presence at the location will give you information. A set of golf clubs or picture of a sailboat on the wall provide ample opening for a discussion related to those activities.

Even the person that comes to your office has provided at least some information from which you can glean a topic. If the person is from a supply company you might simply state, "I was interested when I heard that you were connected with the XYZ firm. I've always had an interest in ____." Even a person without an appointment brings the fact that they are unannounced, and a good humored opening might be, "This is what I like about the job—tell me how did you decide on me?" Or, you might choose to be more competitive and put the person on the defensive by saying something like, "I suppose I can make some time available now."

If we view the negotiation as a series of interrelated steps, we can ask whether any of the other steps can be facilitated by ice breaking. Ice breaking also provides an opportunity to gather important information in its own right. In other words, an appropriate topic for ice breaking can also produce important information. For example, a general question of "How's business?" if answered may give you important information about time, importance of the subject of negotiation, etc.

PROBLEM 5.1

Assume counsel is negotiating with a lawyer who has flown in from a distant city. Counsel have scheduled an early morning meeting. The following occurs:

LAWYER 1 (L1): Hello, Mr./Ms. _____. Nice to meet you. How was the flight over?

LAWYER 2 (L2): Fine.

L1: Did you just get in?

L2: Yes.

L1: Did you have time to check into the hotel yet?

L2: No.

L1: Would you like my secretary to call and confirm for you?

L2: No, not really. Actually I was hoping to wrap this up and get on the road to catch a flight.

L1: Great. When does your flight leave?

L2: In about two hours.

What are the advantages of such an exchange?

In Problem 5.1, the first lawyer picked a topic that is appropriate for developing rapport with the person. Ensuring their comfort communicates concern for them as individuals and allows them to talk, helping put them at ease. The topic also provides important information that there is a time constraint, and that the other lawyer is confident that a resolution will be reached in fairly short order.

This example also illustrates how the approach must be flexible. Having struck upon this important point, the lawyer might alter the framework, jumping to information bargaining to follow-up on this topic. The lawyer continued to ask questions, making sure that she understood the extent of the time constraint. The lawyer, however, should remember to return to complete the ice breaking and agenda setting.

In addition to gathering information, ice breaking provides an opportunity to begin setting the overall strategy and style of the negotiation. In the above example, the lawyer is clearly setting up a cooperative style. A competitive style could as easily be used by cutting ice breaking short or showing a lack of interest in the other person as an individual. As you begin to set your style, you can evaluate the style of the other side during ice breaking.

Problem 5.1 also gives you a sense of the evaluation process that can go on. Even from the bare transcript, it appears other lawyers may not be responsive to extended ice breaking. The short, yes-no answers may be communicating impatience with a process that is not "all business."

B. Agenda Control: What and How You Will Negotiate

At some point the parties should agree on an agenda for the negotiation. Absent a surprise visit or telephone call, part of the agenda is typically set before the interpersonal contact takes place. In other words, the parties are almost always aware of what they are going to negotiate. The parties may have previously set the agenda by phone, mail, the complaint, indictment, or the like. Even then, however, someone is likely to say as a transition from ice breaking, "Well, I guess we're here to discuss Newman (or the merger/the contract/or the like)." There may also be additions to the agenda based on information you have acquired: "Thanks for sending me that information. I know we set this meeting up to talk about..., but as I went through the information, it looked like maybe we should talk a bit about.... Given what I've seen here, they may help us save some money and give you a better position."

In certain circumstances, what you are to negotiate may well constitute a separate negotiation. On the international level, this can be seen where countries conduct preliminary negotiations before summit meetings on the topics the leaders will actually discuss at the summit. This also occurs in legal contexts. In a merger or acquisition negotiation the parties may disagree over whether a basic issue is even negotiable. Where the parties sit down to discuss merging personnel policies, the acquiring business may be in such a strong position that it insists that whether the acquired business changes its policy is not a negotiable issue, but only when it will do so. Likewise in many plea negotiations, guilt on at least some criminal charge is a given.

As important as agreeing on what to negotiate, is how you are to negotiate the issues. Research indicates a correlation between success and ability to control how the negotiation proceeds. This makes sense if you accept the fact that a systematic approach to negotiation results in better settlements. If, as we will discuss, information bargaining must precede making an offer, then the party who ensures that it can information bargain before being forced to make a proposal will likely do better.

Saying you need to control the agenda is one thing, but how do you do it? Perhaps the most obvious way to try to gain control is to simply begin the negotiation the way you want to and assert control. Using the eleven-step process, start ice breaking, state your agenda, and then start information bargaining, as in the following example:

> LAWYER 1 (L1): That sounds like a great vacation. You must have had fun.
>
> ANSWER (A): We sure did.
>
> L1: Well, we better get down to business. I know you are busy, so I don't want to take up any more time than necessary. I have found that the best way to proceed is if we first make sure we're here to talk about the same thing—the possibility of my client exchanging his testimony against Smith in exchange for a deal on the liquor store charge.
>
> A: That's right.
>
> L1: Good. Then let's do this. I'd like to ask you some questions. Find out a bit about your perspective. After I have had a chance to do that, you can ask me some questions. After I've had a chance to get to know your needs better, then I'll be in a position to see if there is anything we can work out.

Note in this example, defense counsel has basically said that she is: (1) going to set the agenda; (2) going to information bargain; and (3) only then consider whether a proposal is appropriate. This approach helps you deal with the person who attempts to get you to commit to an offer before you have had a chance to discover important information. You can use the same approach for deciding which issues to negotiate. You might approach an angry lawyer as follows:

LAWYER 1 (L1): Mr. Smith, Carol tells me there is a problem. Please come to my office.

LAWYER 2 (L2): I can't believe it!

L1: Can I get you some coffee?

L2: No. You can tell me why my client's got ten years seniority and ends up getting fired while on vacation. This is unacceptable!

L1: I see you are quite angry. Let's talk about it. Tell me what you see as what happened and let's see if we can figure out a way to get your client to understand what has happened and why.

In this example, the lawyer attempted through ice breaking to set a more reasonable tone, as well as to suggest that a problem-solving procedure is appropriate. At the same time, the lawyer has suggested that the issue to be negotiated is to explain to opposing counsel's client what has happened and why. What the lawyer is trying to keep off the agenda is changing the employment decision.

Controlling the agenda, however, is more than trying to ensure that the process goes through these steps. If you want to be a problem-solver, it means setting the style and keeping it set.

L1: Charlie, our clients have been working together a long time. And, I hear your client wants to reconsider their arrangement; deviate from the terms of the contract. Let's do this. You tell me where your client sees itself in the next few years, what its goals, plans, and desires are. Then let's see how we might meet those needs.

Or, in the case of *Newman v. Popcheck* , the firm's lawyer might try to cast herself as a mediator and say:

It's clear that Ms. Newman and Mr. Popcheck have had a dispute. It seems that to work out an agreeable compromise we need to design a process. That process must sort out what truly happened between the two, what level of intent, negligence, or innocence was involved, and then what each side fairly needs to justly resolve things between them. Why don't we exchange views of what each says happened, and then each can describe what are fair needs that must be dealt with, and finally let's brainstorm some solutions that might help satisfy as many shared, conflicting, and independent needs that we identify?

Controlling the agenda also involves ensuring that where multiple issues are to be discussed, you control the order in which you discuss the issues. For example, you may want to start with a minor issue. You might concede the issue and then set up a fairness doctrine, that it is now the other person's turn to give something. Negotiating the minor issue might also allow you to 1) establish competence to negotiate 2) test the other side's preparation; or 3) develop a pattern and practice of agreement.

Controlling the agenda also means recognizing that you can characterize or quantify an issue in a number of ways, and seek to have the favorable characterization accepted. Take as an example the sale of a large asset. When the lawyer negotiates with a potential buyer, the actual price can be set using a number of values: depreciation, appreciation, return of investment, need to get rid of the asset, need of the customer to have the asset, appraised value, or some combination of these. Effective agenda control means getting the discussion to proceed using the valuation method most favorable to you, or at least getting the most using the valuation system the other side prefers. The effective negotiator will be prepared to argue the appropriateness of each such characterization and may even be able to show how several of these methods arrive at the same favorable result.

Preliminaries to a negotiation are frequently lost opportunities to lay the groundwork for a successful setting. The above discussion has shown how you can use even the small talk at the start of a negotiation to your advantage, and how to set and control the agenda. We will next turn to the important information-gathering phase of a negotiation.

CHAPTER 6
INFORMATION BARGAINING

Having established the agenda, the negotiation typically moves into an exchange of information stage. This stage of the negotiation requires you to ask yourself: 1) what information do you need to seek; 2) what information do you want to disclose; and 3) what information do you want to hide? Your decisions on these three questions will significantly impact the negotiation's outcome.

PROBLEM 6.1

Given what you know about the distinction between problem solving and adversarial negotiation can you think of any general distinctions between the two approaches when it comes to deciding what to seek, reveal, or hide?

We will not discuss Problem 6.1 at this point. As you read through this chapter, however, see what distinctions there are.

A. What Information Do You Want to Seek?

The adversarial negotiator wants to obtain information that will allow her to determine the other side's bottom line. As we discussed in preparation and planning, the adversarial negotiator seeks to identify information that will allow a reasonable estimate regarding that person's bottom line.

The problem-solver wants to have information so that he can determine the needs, interests, and desires to be met. If these needs, interests, and desires can be identified, the problem-solver is in a position to begin considering and proposing alternative solutions that satisfy both sides.

The range of useful information, of course, depends on the issues being negotiated, though they tend to fall into economic, social, and psychological considerations. For example, in *Newman v. Popcheck, Blink*

& *Denis*, the defendants would like to know what the job market is like for someone with Newman's qualifications, whether Newman is able to sustain herself during protracted litigation, and what her long-range plans are. In the areas of social and psychological considerations there are a number of participant-related factors based on the social psychology of the negotiation process as discussed in Chapter 3. Among these factors are:

Negotiator experience

Although statistical evidence shows that experience alone does not make you a good negotiator, lack of experience may mean you have deficiencies which the other side can exploit, such as lack of confidence or lack of understanding the value of a particular negotiating chip being discussed.

Your own common experience will confirm this. People new to a job are generally less confident. Statements made to this person, such as, "Well, the way we usually handle this is...." can increase this discomfort. When you were new to your job you may have felt that way. Less experienced people with whom you deal probably feel that way as well.

PROBLEM 6.2

Assume you are a prosecutor getting ready to meet with a public defender who has just passed the bar. You are going to discuss the possibility of the public defender's client pleading guilty.

How might an adversarial negotiator use the inexperience of the person with whom they are negotiating to their advantage?

How might an adversarial treat this inexperience differently?

Is there a risk to negotiating with an inexperienced negotiator?

If you are the one that is inexperienced what might you do when dealing with an experienced negotiator?

Looking at the questions raised in Problem 6.2, an adversarial might decide to exploit the possible inexperience by highlighting her own experience. Occasional use of phrases such as, "Your predecessor always did this," or "As you get more experience, you will see that we usually do it this way," may increase insecurity. This insecurity may in turn create a willingness to concede when in doubt.

The problem-solver, on the other hand, might view inexperience as an opportunity to educate the other person, persuading them that there is a better approach than staking out positions. Statements such as, "I've found the best way to approach these negotiations is to _____," may be effective.

The risk of an inexperienced negotiator on the other side is that insecurity does not equate to trust, and trust is what is ultimately required. At some point, the adversarial is going to offer her bottom line, and she will want the other person to believe it is true. If the negotiator is not at her bottom line, then further concessions may have to be made because she was not believed. Even worse, if the negotiator is at his bottom line, there may be no agreement because the other person thinks there is more to be conceded.

Lack of trust is a risk for the problem-solver as well as the adversarial. The problem-solver will need to persuade the other side that problem-solving is appropriate and that ultimately a given proposal is the best for everyone concerned.

Another risk is that the inexperienced negotiator will have precisely the opposite reaction to that anticipated. That is to say, her reaction may be: "I'm new to this and I'd better show I'm tough." Indeed, the social-psychological pressures discussed in Chapter 3 may very well force the inexperienced person to protect herself by being less accommodating.

From the perspective of the inexperienced negotiator, as with any tactic that is used against you, you have to communicate that the attempt to use your inexperience against you will not be effective. This might mean you respond to statements that, "This is the way it is usually done," with the simple statement, "I'll check that out when I get back to the office." When dealing with particularly heavy handed attempts by your opponent to play-up his experience, you may choose to confront the problem directly: "Let's get serious Charlie, I know you have more experience, but that's not going to get you any place."

Time constraints

Research indicates that time pressure tends to increase the likelihood of agreement because bargainers reduce their aspirations, demands, and bluffs. This suggests that when you believe the other side is making excessive demands or is inappropriately trying to bluff you, you might try setting a time limit. When dealing with such a person, simply limiting the time you give them can often be effective: "Charlie, I'm glad we were able to meet. Unfortunately, I'm pressed today and I've got to be at another meeting in fifteen minutes."

Authority to settle

Does the other negotiator have the authority to settle and what are the limits of that authority? When you make a proposal, you need to persuade the other side. Who must you persuade; the person you are dealing with or someone else? If it is someone else, then you need to know this so you can find out what is important to the decision maker.

Anyone who has bought a car knows how effective it can be to separate the negotiator from the person with the real authority. Anytime the salesperson is confronted with an offer from you, they take the offer to the sales manager. Not surprisingly, the salesperson usually comes back saying the sales manager said no. You ask why, and you get a very ambiguous, "It's just not good enough." You then ask to talk to the sales manager, and the salesperson says that is not possible. If this happens, you should probably walk out. How can you effectively negotiate if you cannot find out what the real decision maker values?

PROBLEM 6.3

It is easy to overestimate the value of separating yourself from the ultimate authority. While there may be advantage to the ability to make statements such as, "I'll have to check on that with my people," what are the disadvantages?

The biggest disadvantage in separating yourself from your authority is illustrated by your reaction when the tactic is used against you. A normal reaction is, why aren't you negotiating with the person with authority? Or worse, it may be seen as a bald attempt to manipulate you. Finally, such tactics can seriously affect your credibility. If you constantly refer to a higher authority, your own statements may be less credible: "Why should I believe you now, when on other important issues you said you had to check with your boss?" Likewise, repeated references to a need to check with someone else will often result in repeated pressure by the other side to speak directly to that authority.

Work load of other side

Is the other negotiator so overworked that they have an incentive to resolve the matter quickly?

Who and how paid

Does the other negotiator get a direct reward for this negotiation, and if so, how is it determined? Is the attorney on the staff of the entity or person he represents, or has he been hired on an hourly basis? Is there a motivation to resolve the matter quickly to avoid additional expense? If you are negotiating with a salesperson, are they on commission? Can you find out whether the commission is based strictly on individual sales or does the commission depend on when the sale takes place. For example, salespeople sometimes earn a higher commission for a certain level of total sales within a period, such as a quarter. Would your particular sale move the salesperson up to a higher commission?

Motivation or desire to be a problem-solver or an adversarial

We have discussed how the strategy the parties choose can affect the nature of the negotiation. Which strategy is the other negotiator likely to take: adversarial, problem-solving, or some combination of the two?

B. Where to Get Information

Having decided what information you want, the question then becomes how to gather the information. First, you should remember that because of its critical role, valuable information should be obtained from anywhere, at any time, from any source. One value of viewing the negotiation process as a series of interrelated stages is that while emphasizing that certain things are done at certain points in the negotiation, it also suggests that fruitful opportunities to meet the goals of one stage may present themselves in other stages. Ice breaking is a perfect example of a stage where you can facilitate information bargaining. Topics that might be appropriate to discuss during ice breaking may well be inappropriate at a later time.

Imagine that you have to schedule a negotiation session. It is summer time and you either call the person or see them at some social function. You might take the opportunity to work on the relationship, while also gathering some important information. The conversation might go like this:

LAWYER 1 (L1): Charlie, it's good to see you. I'm sorry I haven't gotten back to you. Your call came in while I was on vacation.

CHARLIE: Did you have a good time?

L1: Great time. Went to the beach. Back now and ready to go. How about you? Any vacation plans?

CHARLIE: Yes. We're taking the family to the beach ourselves.

L1: Great. Where do you go?

CHARLIE: Got a place down on Long Beach. Spend a couple weeks each year down there. Sort of a family tradition. My folks come down. We have a real good time.

L1: Sounds like fun. When you heading out?

CHARLIE: Week from Friday.

In this brief interchange, the lawyer has discovered information that can be used to facilitate the negotiation. The adversarial negotiator might use this information to schedule the negotiation just before the planned vacation, based upon the theory that Charlie would probably want this resolved before vacation so that it does not worry him during vacation. The problem-solver, however, might use this information to set the appropriate relationship and to develop trust by saying, "Well, let's not let our business interfere with your trip. What would be best for you, meeting before or after your vacation?"

In addition to deciding where to get information, you should consider the wide number of sources of information. Sources of information can be categorized as either indirect or direct and as verbal or nonverbal.

An indirect source is any source other than the person with whom you are negotiating. A wide range of possible sources exist, depending on the particular negotiation. The lawyer going to opposing counsel's office indirectly can gain valuable information by viewing the office. In

Newman v. Popcheck, the plaintiff's lawyer may be able to find out information about how highly Popcheck, Blink & Denis values its reputation by asking other lawyers or law firms. Periodicals as common as the daily newspaper may contain financial information about the firm.

Certain information must, of necessity, be obtained indirectly. Take the purchase of a car. Perhaps the most important piece of information that a car purchaser can have is the car's actual cost to the dealer. Once the purchaser knows this, they are in a much stronger position to make an offer. You will probably not get this information directly from the car dealer, but you can obtain it from an indirect source such as one of the many consumer-oriented magazines or books.

Direct methods involve gathering information directly from the person with whom you are negotiating. The most obvious direct source are the statements made by the person with whom you are negotiating. Documentary material, of course, can be just as critical in many negotiation situations.

C. How to Get Information in General

In the context of the give and take of negotiation, you cannot underestimate the importance of gathering information face-to-face. The most common way to get the information is to ask for it. The techniques used to ask for information during a negotiation are fundamentally the same as those used whenever the goal is to acquire information.

D. Types of Questions

As with negotiation in general, information bargaining can be more effective if it is approached systematically. To develop a systematic approach to asking appropriate questions in a negotiation, an understanding of the various types of questions is necessary.

One way to categorize questions is by who selects the topic of the question, the questioner, or the questioned. In general, questions categorized in this way are of four types: open ended, narrow, yes/no, and leading. Which type of question you ask should result in different information being given, both in terms of quantity and quality of information. As with most aspects of interpersonal skills, there is no one correct type of question to ask. Each type of question has its own advantages and disadvantages. By looking at these various advantages and disadvantages, however, you can derive some general principles or suggestions for appropriate questioning.

1. Open-ended Questions

An open-ended question allows the person questioned to select the topic and to discuss what she believes is important about that topic. A classic open-ended question, would be, "Tell me, what's on your mind?" or, "Can you tell me about your plans?"

The advantages of open-ended questions are several. First, and perhaps most importantly, open-ended questions normally get you the most information. The person questioned is urged to talk about whatever is of concern, without restrictions concerning topic or limitations as to length of response. When combined with good active listening skills (discussed below), the open-ended question maximizes acquisition of information.

Because the person is encouraged to talk, open-ended questions also will normally increase the likelihood that a good rapport will develop between the negotiators. The fact that you are willing to listen should communicate your interest and your understanding, thus allowing you to more effectively develop a good working relationship with the other person.

Another major advantage of open-ended questions is that they encourage the other person to identify the important agenda items. Whenever you are negotiating with someone you will usually have a list of topics that you feel are important and need to be explored. If you use an open-ended question before you turn to your own topics, you will increase the possibility that you will find out what is important to the other person. You can then compare what is important to you and what is important to the other person and structure further questions accordingly.

Getting the other person to raise topics can be particularly helpful if you need to explore sensitive items. For example, if you are trying to negotiate the agreement to merge two companies, the scenario might work out as follows:

LAWYER (L1): Let's talk about your needs.

ANSWER (A): Well, they haven't changed much since we last talked. Independence is still critical. The support you folks can provide our company doesn't outweigh the inconvenience of an extra administrative layer we don't want. Central administrations can be lousy in the best of circumstances.

L1: Anything else?

A: Well, to be honest, we need to protect the senior management.

L1: What else?

To the extent that the senior staff is a problem, the other person has raised the issue and at some time it may make it easier for the lawyer to come back and say, "You mentioned the senior staff. Tell me more."

PROBLEM 6.4

Imagine you are going to interview a person to find out as much about their employment as possible.

Imagine you are limited to asking questions that can be answered yes or no, what questions would you ask? What would you anticipate to be the difficulties of this task?

Now imagine you can ask any questions you like, what questions would you ask?

Problem 6.4 provides a useful exercise illustrating the importance of open-ended questions. Take 60 seconds and interview someone about their employment using only questions that can be answered yes or no. The exchange might go something like this:

Q: Do you fix things?

A: No.

Q: Do you make things?

A: No.

Q: Do you provide a service?

A: Yes.

Q: Are you a doctor?

A: No.

Q: Are you a banker?

A: No.

Q: Are you a dentist?

A: No.

Q: Are you a lawyer?

A: Yes.

Q: Do you do criminal work?

A: No.

Q: Do you do civil litigation?

A: No.

Q: Do you do transactional work?

A: No.

The number of questions could go on forever, and you might not get the information you need. Yes or no questions require you to think of every possible piece of information that may be important; a task that is impossible for most people. In this interview example, you need to be able to conceive of every possible variation on employment to be sure that you have all the information. Even when you get a yes for an answer the task simply presents an infinite number of new questions:

Q: Are you employed?

A: Yes.

Q: Have you been employed for more than a year?

A: Yes.

Q: Have you been employed for more than two years in your current job?

A: Yes.

The logical approach, of course, is to ask an open-ended question. Not only will you get more information, you may get information you would never have thought to ask about. Ask your partner open-ended questions and what is likely to happen?

Q: Tell me about your job, would you?

A: Well, I'm a law professor at Emory University School of Law, and have been in law teaching for the past twenty-four years.

Q: Tell me more.

Nonetheless, open-ended questions also present several disadvantages. Because the person will be free to discuss anything, you may get a higher amount of irrelevant information. The level of irrelevant information may be particularly high if the person has brought any psychological needs, such as venting anger. The irrelevant information may also be so great that the person's response becomes unduly long and diffuse. On the other hand, this time and effort may pay off in the form of a better rapport. Further, it should be obvious that we only know information is irrelevant after hearing it. In the midst of a great deal of irrelevant information you may also find one important piece of information. A final disadvantage to open-ended questions is that being general in nature, they allow the person answering more flexibility in avoiding questions. As a result, you may need to follow up with more direct questions.

2. Narrow Questions

A narrow question is a question in which the questioner selects the general subject matter and which aspect of the subject matter is to be discussed. For example in our interview example in Problem 6.4, a narrow question would be, "What courses do you teach?" The biggest advantage of this type of question is that because it is more specifically focused, it increases the likelihood that the questioner will only receive relevant information. Assuming the person questioned is cooperative and not seeking to avoid giving information, a narrow question elicits a higher percentage of relevant information in response.

The disadvantage of a narrow question, however, is that the total amount of information received will be less than with an open-ended question. Narrow questions provide much less opportunity for the other person to raise topics, and thus, if the questioner does not come up with the topic, the topic may not get raised. All the questioner is likely to receive in response to the previous question is information concerning the other courses taught, whereas in our open-ended question we may get additional information. Further, the ability to gather complete information using narrow questions assumes the questioner has sufficient knowledge of all relevant areas of inquiry.

In terms of developing a rapport with the other person, a narrow question may work either as an advantage or a disadvantage. To the person seeking a sympathetic ear, the narrow question provides less opportunity to meet these psychological needs. To lawyers in a hurry, however, the narrow question may be a more efficient use of limited time.

3. Yes/No and Leading Questions

Questions that can be answered yes or no have the advantage of producing high-quality, accurate information (assuming the truthfulness of the person questioned). However, as pointed out with open-ended questions, this accuracy comes at the expense of reducing the quantity of information.

Yes/no questions can also be characterized as being direct and consequently are usually more threatening than more open-ended questions. To certain people this will harm rapport development, increasing anxiety or communicating a perceived lack of "personal interest" on the part of the person asking the questions.

Finally, leading questions are an extreme form of yes/no questions that suggest the answer to the question. The questioner asks, for example, "You're looking for a settlement structure that provides Ms. Newman with a stream of income until she can get a new job, right?" As with yes/no questions, assuming the truthfulness of the person questioned, the quality of information is quite high. Leading questions have, however, all of the disadvantages of yes/no questions plus the additional problem that they facilitate your being misled. To the extent that you indicate to the person what an appropriate response is, the quality of information may actually decrease because you are hearing what the person believes you want to hear, not necessarily the truth as seen by that person.

E. The Funnel Approach to Questioning

The four types of questions discussed above form a continuum going from open ended to narrow. If we view the advantages of each of the question types, we see that certain questions are appropriate for different circumstances. The good questioner uses each type of question when it is appropriate, given the particular advantages of the individual question type. Indeed, it is possible to view fact gathering as starting at either end of a continuum running from open-ended questions and working toward leading questions.

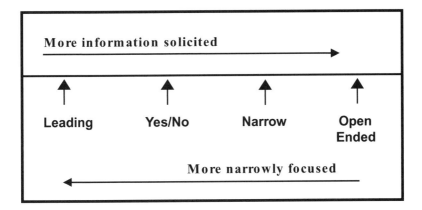

Moving either from leading to open-ended or open-ended to leading questions, the questioner uses all four types, thus taking advantage of each type of question.

Going from open-ended to leading questions is referred to as a funnel approach. As a general rule, most experts recommend that when you seek to systematically gather as much information as possible, you should use a funnel approach.

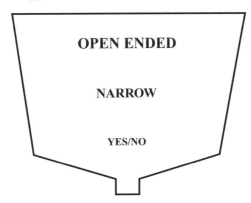

Because open-ended, general questions help develop rapport and a good relationship is something that you usually seek to have throughout the negotiation, a funnel approach seems most appropriate. If we want to systematically approach information gathering, we need to identify the important topics early in the process. Open-ended questions help you to do so. Further, remember that the burden of narrower, more specific questions is that the questioner must have first thought of the general topic. If we want to encourage the other person to suggest information that we ourselves might not cover, it will most likely happen at the beginning of the negotiation in response to open-ended questions.

The advantage of starting with open-ended questions is apparent in light of the risks of narrow questions. If you first cover all the topics you think are important, turning to the other person and asking, "Can you think of anything else?" may be a futile effort. Changing to open-ended questions at the end may not work for two reasons. First, because you have already extensively discussed various topics, the other person may not be motivated to suggest additional topics.

A second and related problem is that questioners "train" people on appropriate response techniques. The questioner who starts out asking yes/no questions subtly tells the person answering that her appropriate role is to provide brief, concise answers. When later asked an open-ended question, the person answering, having played this role throughout the exchange, is unlikely to respond openly. On the other hand, a person you have "trained" to respond to open-ended questions is more likely to keep providing lots of information throughout the exchange.

Remember also, that the narrower, more specific questions, such as "Is Ms. Newman looking for work?" or "Why hasn't she found a new job?" are more threatening, and if asked too soon may hurt the rapport that a cooperative negotiator seeks to achieve. Also, on a practical level, if you remember the specific question early in the interview, you likely will remember it at the end of the interview as well, so you lose little by putting the question off, and you gain much by having patience.

A typical open-ended question starting a funnel approach might be as follows:

LAWYER FOR POPCHECK, BLINK & DENIS (PB&D): Will you bring me up to date about Ms. Newman?

ANSWER (A): Well, she's not happy.

PB&D: Why don't you tell me about it?

A: I don't see the necessity, you've gotten discovery.

PB&D: I'd certainly like to find out where she is today, tell me what you think I need to know to get this thing settled.

A: It's what we've been talking about all along. Her reputation is damaged, she's lost income, her future earning power has been impaired, she's very angry, and, justifiably, she's hurt.

PB&D: Anything else?

A: Yes. She wants PB&D punished.

PB&D: Good. I'd like to talk to you about each of those. I, of course, have some questions myself for you and Ms. Newman.

This person's reaction to the open-ended question, "Will you bring me up to date about Ms. Newman?" is: "She's not happy." The good negotiator, however, will attempt to keep the questioning open-ended and try a different, though still open-ended question: "Why don't you tell me about it?" In this example, the person opens up and we see the common response of people to open-ended questions is talking in lists. With a few questions, the lawyer has elicited a "gush" from the person that contains what appear to be the most important topics they will need to discuss.

The lawyer is now in a position to evaluate what the person has told her. Perhaps more importantly in light of the topics mentioned, as well as topics the lawyer brings to the negotiation, the lawyer can begin to systematically explore various topics. The lawyer can now better decide which topics are important to discuss, how to discuss them, and in what order.

The open-ended question or questions help you identify various topics that are important to explore. Then add other topics, and decide which topics to explore in which order. The good questioner can now choose whether to discuss items mentioned by the other person first, or discuss items on his own agenda, or items that appear important to both sides. If developing a rapport remains a primary consideration, you may, for example, prefer to benefit the other side by meeting his needs first. Each topic, in turn, can be seen as its own funnel for inquiry.

Having decided which topics should be discussed, you should next narrow the inquiry by going to that topic and asking narrower, though still quite open-ended, questions. In reality, then, our funnel analogy is really more accurately described as funnels within funnels. Each new topic creates the beginning of a new funnel of inquiry.

OPEN ENDED QUESTION

To illustrate this further, assume you are meeting with the lawyer of a company that is interested in purchasing a business owned by your client. The purchasing company is new to you and you feel you need to get a great deal of detailed information before your client is prepared to even consider doing business with them. The meeting might proceed as follows:

LAWYER (L): Good. I'd like to talk to you about doing business. I, of course, have some questions about you and your company. Would you tell me about the company?

A: Well we are just expanding into this state. We've seen steady growth over the past few years and find ourselves well positioned to expand.

L: Tell me more.

A: We're family owned. Mr. Duffy's father started the company back in 1950. Duffy senior died about ten years ago and the son took over.

L: What else?

A: I'm not sure what you mean?

L: Tell me some more about the company.

Note here that the lawyer is trying to keep the questions open ended as long as feasible. At some point the person questioned may question the approach and a narrowing of the questions might have to occur.

A: Not much else to say.

L: Tell me about its size, level of sales, that type of thing.

A: As I said, we're growing. We sell to about 50 percent of the hospitals in the tri-state area. Mostly private hospitals.

Once the person no longer "gushes," you might narrow the questions by raising additional topics in question form:

L: What type of products?

L: Service support?

L: How about inventory?

L: Tell me about yourself.

These questions are really just topics the lawyer feels are important, but were not raised by the potential purchaser's lawyer in the "gush." Again, however, you should try to keep it as open ended as possible. If your goal is to acquire as much information as possible, the next step is to pick one of these topics and ask about it in an open-ended way.

L: Awhile back you mentioned you sell to about 50 percent of the hospitals in the tri-state area. Tell me more about that.

Here the lawyer has picked a topic and has begun discussion with a good open-ended question that should maximize information. Additional topics should present themselves and the lawyer can choose which are most important to follow up, seeking more and more specific information, or which can be set aside for later discussion. Indeed, the lawyer may choose to address an entirely new topic, feeling that a more general overview is needed and later return to this topic to "complete the funnel."

Completing the systematic exploration of this topic, or any other topic, will require progressively narrower questions. Continuing our example, here is a series of questions that might follow the earlier questions:

"You've mentioned inventory, tell me about your suppliers."

"Who are they?"

"Tell me about your relationship with them."

103

"Tell me about the financial arrangements."

"What are the regular trade terms offered to the company?

"Are there any special terms involved?"

"Are discounts taken?"

"Are payments prompt?"

"Are any items in dispute?"

"Are contracts or franchises involved?"

"Tell me about those."

"When does it (the contract or franchise) expire?"

Having fully explored the topic, or again choosing to hold off on this level of detail at this time, you can choose a new topic and move through the funnel:

"You mentioned the manufacturing and retail sides, why don't you tell me something about the company's plant and equipment?"

Following the response, necessary follow-up questions (in order of progressing narrowness) may include:

"Are the facilities owned or leased?"

"Who owns the leases?"

"What are the lease terms?

"Any options?"

"Where is the facility located?

"Single purpose or multi-use?"

"Tell me about its operating capacity."

"Is the capacity sufficient for future needs?"

"Anything else you can tell me about the facility?"

Having thus gone through the information in considerable detail, the next stage is to view the information gathered and seek precise details that may not have been mentioned. At this stage, various pre-printed forms are particularly valuable. Also, direct questions, such as those involving costs or discounts, which are perhaps too threatening at the beginning of the negotiation, are less likely to adversely affect the interview.

Using the techniques discussed here during a negotiation raise a number of complicating factors. Most obviously, the person on the other side may not be as cooperative as you would like. You might ask the perfect open-ended question and he may give you short answers. Also, your attempt to get the "gush" may get you only one topic before you are asked to answer a question. The fact that both sides are seeking information is, of course, why we call it information bargaining. What you must keep in mind, however, is that although the gush may take multiple questions and trickle out in what is difficult to see as a gush, you should make every attempt to keep the inquiry as open ended as possible until you are comfortable that all the important topics are on the table. Spending time eliciting the "gush," even when it comes out in a trickle and requires multiple questions, interrupted by your having to answer the other side's questions, is nonetheless critical.

One of the other main difficulties with open-ended questions is that they can be time consuming and in the real world you may not have the luxury of a complete funnel approach. Your initial open-ended questions, however, remain critical. The "gush" sets up the solution to the problem that it takes too much time. Where time is limited, the "gush" is critical because it provides you with the list of topics on which to spend your limited time.

PROBLEM 6.5

Take the example on pages 102–105 relating to the acquisition of a new business deal with a series of related, though separate topics (e.g., management, inventory, etc.). Quite often, the circumstances surrounding your negotiation involve some prior transaction or occurrence. Rather than having a series of topics that you need to explore, there is a chronological event that must be explored. For example, your client may be having difficulty getting a subcontractor to comply with a contractual obligation or the contractor may be trying to renegotiate the completion of the contractual obligation.

What is the equivalent to the funnel approach when dealing with a chronological problem?

An open-ended question that might be appropriate for a chronologically based negotiation is illustrated by the following example:

LAWYER (L): I understand you are having some recent difficulties. Why don't you start at the beginning and take me step-by-step through the problem?

ANSWER: I'm not sure what you mean.

L: Well, why don't you start at the point when you started the project and take me step-by-step through what happened?

During this stage, if you want the person to proceed with a chronology, the next appropriate question may simply be, "Then what happened?" Each event mentioned is the equivalent of the funnel within the funnel. You can begin exploring individual parts of the chronology with such questions as, "You mentioned that on September 5, you talked to the bank. Will you tell me about that?"

Many lawyers have gone to negotiations to resolve litigation that has been going on for years, with massive discovery, and asked only specific questions, only to find out later that the other party had undergone financial setbacks and was on the brink of bankruptcy. Never assume that facts have not changed. A good open-ended question such as, "Bring me up to date," may save you embarrassment later.

F. Information You Do Not Want to Reveal

During a negotiation whenever someone is asked a question the person would prefer not answering, the person questioned has three choices: tell the truth, avoid the question, or lie. Regardless of other considerations, whichever you choose to do, do it affirmatively. Few people will debate that it is inappropriate to lie in a negotiation. While there may be short-term benefits, given the importance of information, lying can ruin your reputation, hurt your credibility, and destroy any long-term relationship you hope to have.

Revealing the information may be the best course. If you choose to do that, do not hesitate. Do it affirmatively. If you are going to be honest about telling the truth, you might as well get the full benefit from it.

Assume Ms. Newman's lawyer is asked:

PB&D: Does Ms. Newman intend to continue the practice of law?

A: Well, uh…she has a number of options.

PB&D: But are there other specific possibilities that she is looking into?

A: Well, she's considering the AG's office.

Here PB&D's lawyer ultimately reveals the information without much struggle, but it appears grudging. The truth comes out, but the lawyer loses credibility because it appears he tried to avoid giving the information. If the information is going to come out, get the benefit of communicating your honesty and forthrightness by stating it affirmatively and then putting the proper spin on the information. For example:

PB&D: Does Ms. Newman intend to continue the practice of law?

A: Her reputation has been so damaged by your clients that her ability to obtain comparable employment in the practice of law is severely limited. She is therefore considering mitigating the damage by going into the public sector.

You may choose to avoid revealing the information short of lying, by blocking or fending off the question. There are standard blocks that are used to fend off questions. Take the question from a prospective employee: "What's your standard salary package for new staff?" One type of block is to leave the questioner with the assumption that the question was answered:

We've never had an arrangement quite like this. You can't really say we have a standard package.

A second type of block is to narrow the focus of the question, in this instance perhaps focusing on the word "standard." The answer might be:

We really don't have a standard package because each staff member is treated as an individual. That's the kind of hospital we pride ourselves on being. Now, I guess what I'd like to hear from you is….

A third type of block is to restate the question to your liking:

You mean is there a salary package that we always provide no matter who the staff member is and what the relationship is like? We don't have one. Now, I guess what I'd like to hear from you is….

A fourth block is to destroy the desire for follow-up questions:

> You mean is there a package we always establish no matter who the staff member is and what the relationship is like? Of course, not. For example, let's take a person with 10 years experience with a major metropolitan hospital, already living in the area, with the ability to start immediately. That person is quite different from the person with limited experience, and the need to provide strong supervision and advanced training. Now, I guess what I'd like to hear from you is....

A final common block is simply to answer the question that was asked. Too often the question is imprecise, not really asking for the information intended. Nevertheless, the person being questioned hears the question, realizes the intent behind it, and usually answers what was intended, rather than what was actually asked. In our example, the person asked what was the standard package. They probably intended to ask something like, "Given what you already know about me and my experience, what are you prepared to offer me in terms of a specific package?" That is a tough question to avoid. What was actually asked, however, was what is the standard package? An effective block to this imprecise question may be simply to answer the question asked, not the question that was intended to be asked: "We don't have a standard one."

To be effective, the block must be stated affirmatively and be followed with a question of your own so as to shift the initiative from the questioner and avoid follow-up questions.

The real risk of blocks is that if it is perceived by the questioner as a block, you have effectively communicated that you are hiding harmful information. While the questioner may not have the specific information, the person will realize that you would have revealed it if it helped you. Added to this, the questioner may begin to question your credibility. Use blocks carefully.

As with all aspects of negotiation, you must view the use of blocks not only from your perspective, but also from the perspective of the other person. In other words, whether or not you use blocks, the other person might, and you should be aware of them. After asking a question you must train yourself to listen not only for the substance of the answer, but also to determine whether or not the answer is responsive. If the answer is not responsive, it may be a block.

If we look at the standard types of blocks in the *Newman* negotiation, you might ask: "Does Newman intend to continue to practice law?" The range of blocks might include:

— "She does not have any current employment."

— "She's keeping her options open to all possibilities."

— "You mean has she given up on the idea that she should be employed in a major law firm with the potential for a salary in the high six figures?"

— "Any decision Ms. Newman makes will depend on a number of considerations."

How you handle people who fail to reveal information varies depending on the circumstances. In certain circumstances, doing nothing is appropriate. Simply remember that their refusal to disclose has its own meaning and use that information as you would any other. For example, any of the blocks just covered clearly indicate the person is uncomfortable making the first offer. This suggests they are unsure what the value of their side should be and you should encourage them to expect a lower value.

In some circumstances you may have made the block easy, and you should rephrase your question specifically. Here, the question might be rephrased, "Is Ms. Newman looking for work other than the private practice of law?" In certain circumstances where you have a sufficiently strong relationship that will withstand it, the appropriate response to a block might be to confront the person: "Boy, Charlie, I haven't heard such bologna since the Presidential debates. Give me an answer." Where the relationship with the person is no longer important the confrontation may also rise to a personal challenge and the anxiety may result in information: "You didn't really answer the question, let me rephrase it...."

Often variations on the same question can get you information that was previously blocked. For example, "Where has Ms. Newman applied for work?"

Where the other party uses the "There are too many variables to answer that question" block, your best response is probably to take each variable and ask how it affects the answer.

G. Impediments to Questioning

Do not assume that what appears to be a lack of cooperation by someone with whom you are negotiating is always motivated by an attempt to manipulate you. Questioning in a negotiation will not always proceed smoothly. The other person may be nonresponsive or talk about tangential points. Their need for information may be so strong that it runs directly contrary to your attempt to systematically gather information.

Psychologists have identified a series of reasons why people being questioned do not provide clear, accurate, and organized information. While this book is certainly not a treatise on psychology, it helps you to understand the negotiation dynamic if you know some of the more common inhibitors. Only after identifying what is inhibiting the communication process are you able to identify a solution.

1. Ego Threat

Self-esteem is a critical factor in most people's psychological make-up. People will often avoid providing information which they believe will place them in a negative image in front of others and hurt their ego. For example, a person who has had a series of financial reversals may be unwilling to provide accurate information for fear that the person will view her as incompetent or foolish.

2. Result Threat

People refuse to give information because they fear it will hurt their attempt to get the result they want. Take, for example, a merger and acquisition negotiation. Business reversals may pose a personal threat, because the fear that the acquiring business in a merger and acquisition will refuse favorable terms as a result of the information.

3. Role Expectation

Society puts individuals into certain roles and others expect that people will act according to these roles. In a legal negotiation this is most apparent in how the respective lawyers view their roles. The lawyer who believes, or has a client who believes, that lawyers are supposed to be tough, aggressive negotiators, may simply not realize that an alternative exists. The problem goes beyond mere intimidation. If one lawyer views negotiation as a debate over positions, he may be unwilling to give the opposing counsel a correct statement of underlying needs because he expects the opponent to use it against him. Indeed, if you perceive your role as a cooperative problem-solver, this misperception can sometimes lead to deadlock, because your attempts to get opposing counsel to open up and talk freely may be met with one- or two-word answers.

Perceived inequality of status can likewise affect your negotiations. If you are negotiating with an older lawyer, you may have to fight the reluctance to defer to the person merely because of status. Similarly, you must not let the person's status intimidate you so you do not ask the questions you need to ask or allow the other lawyer to avoid answering the questions you have asked.

4. Perceived Irrelevancy

If one of our goals is to obtain accurate, relevant, and reliable information, problems can result from the other person having a different view of what is relevant information. A person may simply not mention information because they think it is irrelevant. Further, if you seek what the person perceives as irrelevant information, they may react negatively, hurting rapport and inhibiting your attempts to acquire information.

5. Greater Need

The other person's goals for the negotiation often are such that there is little that can be done to simultaneously meet both your goals and his. Imagine a situation where you are talking to a lawyer for the company your client would like to acquire. You may be asking for a great deal of specific information that you can then use to justify a specific proposal, yet in what is clearly intended to be a cooperative, problem-solving negotiation, your opponent avoids answering and talking about what the name of the merged company will be. It may be that this lawyer's client has a need that is greater than the money part of the deal, such as a desire to have his name memorialized.

In *Newman*, if Popcheck et al is trying to pin down the financial needs of Ms. Newman, and her attorney keeps talking about vindication, it is a pretty clear indication that Newman has a higher need. Two things therefore follow. First, if you are to avoid deadlock, you may have to temporarily give up what you are trying to do to allow you to address this greater need. Second, if you recognize the problem as the opponent having a greater need, you may take advantage of this, especially if your opponent's need is unimportant to you. For example, if Ms. Newman has a greater need for vindication than money, this indicates she might settle for less money in exchange for a public apology. If it turns out that the apology is not an issue for your client, you can trade your meaningless bargaining chip (an apology) for a blue chip (less money).

6. Forgetting

Human beings forget. Related to forgetting, the person being questioned may be confused or have incomplete memory. Memory is made up of several factors, including not only the original perception at the time, but that perception modified over time by external factors. For example, a lawyer's relationship with a client may be influenced not simply by personal contacts, but by statements of other people who have dealt with the lawyer in the past.

7. Time and Money

Time is a significant factor in most business relationships. A busy person may give less information in order to avoid the added cost of a longer negotiation. The person may feel time spent with you is time more profitably spent elsewhere. Trying to negotiate a small claim, for example, may be complicated by the fact that opposing counsel believes she is too busy to discuss such mundane issues as your "little accident." Your task will be to recognize this as a problem and conduct the discussions in a way to minimize this attitude's effect.

H. Techniques to Motivate

You can deal with problems inhibiting information gathering in several ways. While none of these are foolproof, they do provide a range of techniques which can be used to encourage the other side to provide information.

1. Education

One of the most effective, and perhaps least used, techniques to get a person to provide information is to educate the person. Quite often, problems which inhibit the questioning result from the person not having a systematic view of the process and not knowing that anything is wrong. By educating the person, you can often reap immediate rewards.

The person giving short answers to open-ended questions, or the person who jumps from one topic to the next, might benefit from a simple explanation as to the process you would like to follow:

I realize we have a limited amount of time to spend today so I thought we might proceed as follows. I've found that I can most efficiently use your time if I start off with some general questions and have you tell me as much about each topic as you can. I can then go back and ask you for any additional specific information I need. Then we can answer any questions you may have.

2. Cost-Benefit Analysis

Education will often also help with problems such as loan or ego threat by providing a cost-benefit analysis. For example:

It must be difficult talking about these business reversals. As difficult as it is, we need this information. In fact, having it is less harmful than not having it, because we can't resolve this outstanding problem without some very specific information.

3. Empathetic Understanding, Recognition, and Catharsis

Sometimes people come to a negotiation with psychological needs requiring empathy, sympathy, catharsis, or recognition. Often the best technique to get beyond these needs is to provide the empathetic/ sympathetic ear, or the chance for the person to have the catharsis. For example, providing Ms. Newman a forum to vent past grievances may be extremely helpful to your position if you represent Popcheck, Blink & Denis. By sitting back and listening you may be able to convince her that things have changed. Further, you can provide recognition by statements such as, "This is important information," or "You're providing me with a good background here."

4. Active Listening

Active and passive listening techniques will both foster the giving of information by the person and help maintain an appropriate rapport. Listening techniques range from neutral or passive to directive or active. Passive or neutral responses to a person's statement convey little information to the person and are designed to simply indicate that the lawyer is still listening and the person should continue talking. Active or directive responses communicate information, or the lawyer's interpretation of the person's response and, therefore, may direct the person toward new topics or indicate to the person that they need to clarify information already provided. The following are common listening techniques you may find helpful.

Silence

Silence can be one of the most effective neutral probes for information. People are socialized to abhor silence. We turn on radios without really listening to them; we hum; we have music in elevators. Given silence, most people will seek to fill it with noise. This is as true in the interview as it is in life in general. If you do not speak, chances are that the other person will. Simply waiting as little as a second after the person drops her voice indicating she has finished may be enough to encourage her to continue. This technique is particularly helpful following an open ended question.

"Mm-hm"

Statements such as "Mm-hm," "yes," or "I see," following a comment by the person are neutral probes and communicate that you are listening intently to what is being said. When followed by silence, the statements encourage the listener to keep talking.

Restatement

A slightly more directive listening technique is restating what the person says. Restatement shows the person that you are listening; in fact, listening so intently you are able to repeat the person's exact words. For example:

> L1: So after the last staff meeting they decided to seriously discuss this attempt to control emergency room activity.

> L2: The decision to seriously discuss the attempt to control emergency room activity came after the last staff meeting?

Restatement is more directive than "Mm-hm" because it may communicate greater interest on the part of the lawyer and, therefore, indicate to the person that you need more information on this topic. It is particularly effective in bridging between combative and competitive exchanges and a more empathetic and problem-solving approach. If a party can demonstrate empathy and understanding by accurately summarizing the opposition's positions and demands, then the opposition may feel that they can trust you, listen more completely to your side of the case, and work together to devise a win-win strategy for resolution.

Clarification

Asking for a clarification is more directive than restatement. For example:

L1: So after the last staff meeting we decided to seriously discuss this attempt to control the emergency room.

L2: The decision came after the staff meeting. I'm not sure I understand. Was there a connection between the meeting and the decision to change procedure?

Reflection

Reflection can also help. With reflection, you add an interpretation to the person's statement. Because the interpretation contains information about your perceptions, the statement may be quite directive.

L1: So after the last staff meeting we decided to seriously discuss this attempt to control the emergency room.

L2: The decision came after the staff apparently expressed concern over the current condition of the emergency room.

Not only facts, but feelings can be reflected:

L1: So after the last staff meeting we decided to seriously discuss this attempt to control the emergency room.

L2: It sounds like there is some anger about the control.

Reflection can also be a key bridge to problem-solving. If catharsis is to be gained, the person with the emotion needs to feel listened to. Reflection then may lead the opposition to be able to feel more able to put the emotion aside and deal more objectively with the situation. (Of course, others may worry that encouraging the expression of strong emotion will only make a party more wedded to his position. The usefulness of reflection is very context- and party-specific, and is, therefore, a more risky active listening technique than the others listed above.

I. Nonverbal Communication

In addition to verbal communication you should be as aware of nonverbal communication in a negotiation as you are in an interview. Nonverbal information is often more valuable, because it is often not intended to be communicated and therefore has a higher reliability. Indeed, professional negotiators refer to such unintentional communication (whether verbal or nonverbal) as "leakage."

A complete review of nonverbal communication is beyond the scope of this work. A brief review, however, should emphasize its importance. Nonverbal communication can be divided into four types: chronemics; kinesics; proxemics; and paralinguistics. With regard to each of these, experts have drawn various conclusions, but four generalities particularly apply in legal negotiation and deserve special mention.

First, many experts believe that the effectiveness and usefulness of words tend to be overestimated. Some experts estimate that as much as sixty percent of all important messages are passed nonverbally. An awareness of nonverbal communication is therefore critical for interpersonal communication. Second, not only is a great deal of information passed nonverbally, certain types of gestural language cannot be communicated by words.

A third important point is that some nonverbal information is a physiological response to stress and therefore may be a more accurate indication of information. Blushing, for example, may be a more accurate indication of embarrassment than any spoken words. Finally, many psychologists believe that there is always what they refer to as message redundancy. In other words, people communicate the same information in multiple ways. A person who is uncomfortable in a particular situation may both wrap his arms around himself and blush. Given that nonverbal communication is subject to interpretation (a person wrapping their arms around themselves may simply be cold), message redundancy allows us to search for a confirming interpretation of a message we think we are receiving nonverbally.

1. Leakage

Almost anything the other side does may leak information. For example, when the other party is coming in from out of town, has arrived the night before, and shows up at your office with a suit bag, she "leaks" information that she has checked out of the hotel. This gives you information that as the negotiations take longer and longer, the other side may need to quickly resolve the negotiation or change their travel plans. The additional trouble may not make a critical difference, but it may put additional pressure on the other side.

Like any information, you can actively seek leakage. Take our previous example, where the lawyer has to sell a large asset. During the ice-breaking stage, the lawyer may bring up the question of whether an out-of-town buyer needs hotel accommodations in order to see if the buyer will "leak" whether they have plans to stay overnight. The lawyer may then determine the time frame with which they have to work.

Two types of leakage merit special mention because of their re-occurrence in negotiation after negotiation. First, there is the leakage resulting from waffle words. These are words that communicate a lack of a firm position. How many times have you or the person you are nego-tiating with said something like, "We are looking for something between ten and fifteen?" You usually cannot ask for a range in a negotiation. The lawyer hearing this range should assume that either ten or fifteen is acceptable, depending on which is more favorable to the lawyer. The only time you should speak of ranges is when you attach conditions to explain the range, such as, "We want ten to fifteen depending on wheth-er...." Also, using the term "looking for" leaks the person will take less. If, for example, ten were the person's real bottom line, they likely would have been more affirmative and emphatic saying, "We want ten."

A concession pattern can also leak information. As you approach your bottom line or commitment point, concessions tend to get smaller and smaller and faster and faster. If you listen and keep track of the size and speed of concessions, you may get a sense of whether the latest concession is truly the bottom line.

2. Chronemics

Chronemics, or the use of time to communicate, can take many forms. A lawyer can communicate a great deal about the importance of the negotiation based on his use of time. If he squeezes the negotiation in between two other meetings he obviously does not highly value the negotiation. Also, a lawyer who is chronically late communicates infor-mation concerning his perception of the relationship.

3. Kinesics

Kinesics is the use of the body to communicate. Interestingly enough, researchers indicate that most people focus on the face of the other person in an interview. They also believe the face reveals the most accurate information. Research also indicates, however, that a listener tends to watch the other speaker's eyes more closely than a speaker watches the listener's. The lesson from the research seems clear. We should continue to be aware of the face as a primary source of information, but be aware that some non-verbal information may be missed by failure to watch the entire body.

Examples of kinesics are familiar to most people. With respect to body posture, slouching may connote lack of concern or defeat. Feet movements or tapping or swaying of legs and feet may show nervousness. Hand movements, such as placing the hand over the mouth when talking, may show the speaker is unsure about the statement being made. Facial expressions can communicate a wide range of information including disgust, anger, sadness, and joy. Eye movements are also significant, such as rolling or darting eyes showing disbelief or anxiety.

4. Proxemics

Proxemics is using the environment to communicate. We have already discussed a major environmental control in the negotiation when we discussed where the negotiation should take place, including arranging furniture and people's ability to control intrusions into their space.

Psychologists also tell us that objects such as flower vases and abstract sculpture in a negotiation setting tend to facilitate informality and cooperative behavior. Books in a negotiation setting tend to inhibit informality and cooperative behavior. Round tables increase informality and feelings of closeness.

Proxemics is at play in other contexts as well. As with all non-verbal communication, proxemics is subject to interpretation and the interviewer needs to seek confirmation of the information. For example, when you are greeted at the door (or when you greet someone) do they move toward you indicating they are pushy, aggressive, assertive, or anxious to get to know you? Or do they (or you) step back, indicating they are welcoming, passive, or easily manipulated?

Furniture placement within a room can either facilitate or inhibit communication. As a general rule, locating large objects between people decreases communication. If you wish to develop a cooperative, caring relationship, it makes sense not to interview the person from behind a large desk. Sitting side by side is perhaps best. On the other hand, in many cultures being physically close can inhibit communication. As with most interpersonal skills, flexibility in proxemics is an advantage. A furniture arrangement that lets you choose how close to sit can facilitate communication. In addition, the type of furniture can impact the flow of communication. Chairs with wheels can help communication,

Adversarial Information Exchange

- Open-ended questions design to get the opponent to reveal
- Precise follow-up questions design to pin down and discover the extent of the opponent's vulnerabilities
- Blocking strategies for limiting exchange of vulnerable information
- Use agenda control
- Answer a question with a question
- Over answer a question
- Under answer a question
- Answer a related question
- Use a provocative non-sequitor
- Exchange vulnerabilities but make opponent go first
- Rule a question out of bounds

Integrated Approach to Informati

- Start as a cooperative adversarial
- If not, stay adversarial till deadloc
- Teach or persuade opponent to us exchange
- If agrees and you trust opponent listed above

ER 7

NGE

ors will suggest a solution to what the solution an offer, a demand, or a number of common elements. If to accomplish with your proposal, el there are two goals. First, you s fair, just, and equitable, and one xtent possible. Common sense tells the proposal meets these criteria,

ortant goal exists. You must also ave nothing else to offer. Whether competitive adversarial that "The e more!" or in the terms of a prob- think of a better solution," you will ide believes that, despite the offer's vailable.

goal is that you must persuade the g else, knowing that down the road You must make the proposal in a not undercut your credibility when arial) you make a concession or (as proposed solution.

Next, we will address the a the exchange.

uasion

thing

ition is an essential element of any . To give your proposal credibility just, and equitable, as well as rea- unsupported proposal does little to persuade the other side of anything other than that you picked a particular number or other solution out of the air. If you will pick one number out of the air why won't you pick another number more favorable to the other side? Reasons help you persuade the other side that the proposal is fair, just, and equitable and that you are not prepared to offer more.

2. Objective Criteria Arguably Beyond Your Control

Perhaps the most important component to persuasion in negotiation is the use of objective criteria that are arguably beyond your control. Objective criteria are more persuasive than subjective. When the defense lawyer is negotiating with plaintiff's counsel and says, "We won't pay more than $70,000 because it is fair," the statement is unpersuasive. Fair to whom, based on what criteria? Wouldn't $75,000 be fairer? Saying "$75,000 is all I can offer because of restrictions by the insurance company," is marginally more persuasive. A semi-objective reason—they won't let me do it—supports this statement, but the reason is not beyond the control of the lawyer's client.

Saying "$75,000 is our offer—it makes sense given that we settled a similar claim for $75,000 last week," is much more persuasive. Here, the statement is supported by an objective indicator of the "market" price, which is arguably beyond defense counsel's control because it is either set by the nebulous concept of "the market" or by other plaintiffs' attorneys.

Even proposals involving something less quantifiable than money, such as work schedules, are more persuasive when they are objective.

> Labor Lawyer: The schedule is simply not fair. Look at the schedules over the past three months. During that time union employees have consistently been denied overtime on weekends. Here, let me show you....

Anybody with an adjustable rate mortgage, home equity line, or credit card has experienced discomfort over the bank's ability to control interest rates. This discomfort is in part related to this issue of objective criteria. Customers frequently reject pricing on such adjustable rate loans if based on prime plus some percentage point. One possible reason for this rejection is that, while prime is objective, the customer may not perceive it as beyond the bank's control. The offer does not sound fair, just, and equitable, because there may be an underlying fear that the bank will arbitrarily increase prime. Basing the rate on something like the cost of funds to the bank (such as United States Treasury Bills), however, may sound more persuasive because, whether correct or not, customers perceive it as less subject to the bank's control. The fact that the bank's prime is driven by cost of funds, and that all pricing whether based on prime or cost of funds is ultimately controlled by market forces, is irrelevant to this customer. A rate based on the cost of funds is more attractive because it appears beyond the control of the bank.

Often, the most difficult part of making a persuasive statement is identifying the objective criteria that can be used to justify a subjective issue. Imagine the lawyer engaged in setting up a health maintenance organization or managed care facility. The lawyer must negotiate with various private physician groups to get them to join the new organization. The lawyer might have problems persuading a potential group practice that the proposed business relationship actually will provide a better level of service for the group's patients. Lawyers representing the promoters of the new business entity must identify objective measures of patient satisfaction and quality of service to support their proposal. Statistics concerning patient turnover, new business, or the like might be persuasive in this example.

In a merger or acquisition negotiation, there might be an issue of distrust between two previously competing businesses. Identifying a way to quantify trust can be quite challenging, but pointing to specific trust-building measures in other acquisitions may be helpful. For example, the acquiring company's showing that it has a good record for employee retention following an acquisition can be objective and persuasive. Also, making a specific commitment public by way of a press release may make the commitment seem beyond the control of the negotiator and therefore more permanent and consequently more persuasive.

The connection between effective client counseling and the ability to develop objective criteria should be apparent. Having the client identify what he would like to accomplish is clearly an essential step. Getting the client to help you identify the potential rationales for why that result is appropriate is equally important.

PROBLEM 7.1

In *Newman v. Popcheck*, Ms. Newman has indicated that her primary goal is to get as much money from Popcheck, and Popcheck, Blink & Denis as possible. What objective criteria, arguably beyond your control, can be used to justify a particular high settlement?

Assume instead that Ms. Newman has indicated that money is not nearly as important as getting a new job, having sufficient cash flow during the job search and get an apology. What objective criteria, arguably beyond your control, can be used to justify a particular high settlement?

Identifying objective criteria, of course, depends on the particular facts associated with a negotiation. However, the criteria must be something valued by the person with whom you are negotiating. For example, in the above problem, a reasonably safe working premise (that we will of course check out during information bargaining) would be that Popcheck, Blink & Denis value money and reputation. To maximize the amount of money Ms Newman can demand, a number of criteria suggest themselves. Clearly, jury verdict research is an important criterion. Past jury verdicts are both objective and arguably beyond the control of the parties, and the more similar the case, the more persuasive the analogy. A typical persuasive statement based on jury verdicts might go:

Our client has authorized me to accept lower figures to settle this case. Let me explain how we have arrived at this figure. We have done extensive research on verdicts in these types of cases. Independent of our own research we have consulted with Jury Verdict Research, Inc. I have its report here, as well as a listing of similar cases involving sexual harassment against professional women. You will see that the verdicts range between 375,000 and 1.3 million dollars. Given the public nature of this dispute and the fact that Ms. Newman is in the higher income bracket among the plaintiffs in these cases (the 1.3 million was a physician, we have a $450,000 verdict for an associate), at least a $450,000 verdict is likely. We recognize, of course, that between trial and appeals we are looking at four years to recover that amount. So we are willing to reduce it to its present value. Our accountant tells us that the present value of $450,000 in four years is $375,000. We estimate that we will also save $45,000 in litigation expenses. Subtract that and you get $330,000.

Jury verdicts are not the only objective criteria. Experts in an appropriate field often provide value data upon which to base offers and persuasive statements. Indeed, choosing different criteria can result in vastly different offers.

3. Argumentation

One of the best analyses of what makes arguments persuasive is from the field of rhetoric. We add to and modernize the description of these classical rhetorical elements as follows.

a. Be Detailed

The more detail you provide to support your position, the more persuasive it will usually be. The statement, "The schedule is fair because it is consistent with what is happening at other comparable businesses," is objective and arguably beyond management's control. Compare, however, the statement:

> Before we made the schedule, I checked around. I checked the other comparable employers. At Metropolitan the average amount of overtime for workers is forty hours for the last six months. During that same period the average has been thirty-five hours for City as well as University hospital. Here we see that each union member in this department has averaged thirty-six hours during the last six months. Here, let me show you our schedule....

The second statement has the same rationale as the previous example, but it is more persuasive because it contains detailed information about how the schedule was created and compares to others.

Detail often requires proof. For example, when we justified $330,000 based on jury verdict research in the previous scenario, the statement was quite detailed and the lawyer was prepared to provide documentary proof that she had not just pulled the figures out of the air. Providing copies of the economist's report (as well as his curriculum vitae) might be helpful.

b. Multi-Dimensional Reasoning

As a general rule, more supporting reasons make your position more persuasive. If you can show that no matter which way you look at a problem the solution always seems to be the same, the solution will more likely be perceived as fair, just, and equitable. A simple car negotiation involving the purchase of a used car illustrates the point:

BUYER: I'll give you $15,000 for your car.

SELLER: Too low, the ad says $16,000, and I'm not going any lower.

BUYER: But, wait, look at this. I checked the blue book value on this car. Here, see for yourself. The wholesale price listed is $16,500, the retail price is $17,000. But, you need to, according to the book, subtract $750 for high mileage. That makes the price $15,750. Then you have to figure the tires need to be replaced, that's another $150 apiece so we're at $15,150. Bottom line is I'm also going to have to have the engine looked into and you have said yourself there hasn't been any brake work. That's bound to be needed, so $15,000 is right.

SELLER: I don't know....

BUYER: $15,000 also makes sense from what I see in the market. Look at these other advertisements. Here's the same make and model, a year newer for $17,000. Here's the same make and model, but a year older for $14,500. Also, you are the one who told me the dealer wouldn't give you what you thought the car was worth in trade-in. You'll do better with my $15,000 than with the dealer's trade-in value. Don't forget that if you take it today, you can cancel the insurance right away, that will save you a couple of bucks, and you avoid the hassle and expense of trying to find someone else.

Here, the persuasive statement points out five reasons why $15,000 is the correct price: 1) blue book value; 2) market price based on other advertisements; 3) can't get a better price at dealer; 4) time savings; and 5) money savings. Individually, each of the arguments have a different persuasive force. The blue book argument is objective and beyond the control of the parties. It is also highly detailed. The blue book argument, however, has a major flaw in that the buyer does not explain picking the wholesale price as a starting point; that is not really beyond the control of the party. The other advertisement argument is objective, but lacks detail. The final three arguments are beyond the buyer's control, but lack detail and objectivity. Taken together, however, they are more persuasive than taken alone, and create a more compelling rationale.

The same affect can be used in a number of situations. For example, assume the lawyer's client is seeking to sell a multimillion dollar item:

BUYER (B): You're the seller. What's the bottom line?

LAWYER (L): Two million dollars.

B: How did you arrive at that figure?

L: It seemed a fair price in light of existing circumstances. We know replacement cost is $2.3. Original cost was $1.75 The price should be somewhere in between.

B: What about depreciation?

L: I look at depreciation this way. This is more like a vintage car than a Chevy. Initially there is going to be some depreciation, but with rising costs its value has got to increase. Its value won't catch up to a new unit, but kept in condition it could well never go below its original cost and may increase in value as well.

B: But what's magic about $2.0 million?

L: It's not magic. Look at it from my perspective. This unit is an investment. A reasonable return on an investment like this would be 10 percent a year and that's $250,000 for the past two years. Do the math, without compounding, $1.75 million plus $250,000 is $2 million. Two million is also consistent with the recent appraisal we had on the unit.

Here the lawyer has used replacement costs, appreciation based on original cost, return on investment, and an appraisal to support his position. Each is objective and arguably beyond the control of the lawyer. For example, she did not create the concept of appreciation, it exists in the real world. Clearly, some of the rationales are more beyond the control of the lawyer than others. The lawyer did, after all, pick the appreciation value and probably also selected who was going to be the appraiser. Taken as a whole, however, the arguments are more persuasive than taken individually.

c. Balanced Arguments

Proposals have to be fair, just, and equitable to both sides. Any rationale that merely focuses on one side is inherently less persuasive. No matter how objective, detailed, and multi-dimensional the argument you make, if you focus solely on the needs, interests, and desires of your client, the other person will react with, "What's in it for me? This deal needs to meet my needs as well." The argument requires, therefore, a balanced rationale that shows how it meets both sides' needs, interests, and desires.

However, the argument also cannot focus solely on the other side's goals. A persuasive statement that never shows what you get out of the proposal may cause the other person to question your credibility. The negotiation involves meeting both sides' goals. If you fail to articulate the reasons the proposal meets your needs, the person with whom you are negotiating may think you have hidden something and are afraid to reveal some benefit you seek.

d. Emphatic and Emotional

If you do not believe in your position, why should anyone else? You must communicate conviction by being appropriately emotional and emphatic. While this does not mean tears, it does mean being affirmative and not equivocating. Compare the following statements.

Wrong:

The most we are willing to offer is in the neighborhood of $300,000.

We're looking at $300,000 and the client does not want to make an apology.

Correct:

The client will pay only $300,000, the terms must be confidential, and there certainly won't be an apology.

Wrong:

I don't know, it's unlikely I could get approval for that offer.

Correct:

That offer is unacceptable.

e. Certain Arguments Must Be Subtle

Despite the fact that most arguments are persuasive when they are detailed, some arguments are actually less effective with detail. Take a variation on merger and acquisition negotiation:

L1: You're buying, what's the bottom line?

L2: Six million dollars.

L1: How did you arrive at that figure?

L2: It seemed fair in light of existing circumstances. We know book value is $6.85 million. Our start-up costs would be $3 million. And we value the goodwill at $1 million. That's $4 million. The price should be somewhere in between.

L1: What about my client's experience?

L2: That's a separate issue. We will agree to continue his employment at $100,000. And besides, let's face it. Your client needs to sell. From what I can tell, you don't have much choice. From what you've told me there's no other purchaser available and he doesn't have the resources to compete.

Put yourself in the position of the client who is to be acquired. How would you feel if you were in the position and this argument were made to you? Would there be a chance that you would react negatively on a basic personal level, and decide, no matter how badly you wanted to sell the business, you would not be so blatantly pushed around?

Certain arguments simply cause people to act in a non-rational manner. They force people to take action, as discussed in Chapter 3, not because the action takes them toward their rationally determined goal, but because of some social-psychological reason. The threat to the seller's ego by such a direct, personal challenge might force the seller to walk out. When it is likely that an argument will precipitate non-rational behavior and you are confident the other person will make a detailed argument to himself, the argument should be subtle. Change the last paragraph in our previous example to:

> Let me tell you, we appreciate your willingness to talk to us and have no intention of taking advantage of today's tight market conditions.

You can be assured the other party will fill in the details of that tight market, including the fact that no alternative purchaser exists. In fact, you could probably be even more subtle and not mention the tight market at all. If the seller's need and limitation of options has already been mentioned as part of the information bargaining, you can be confident that the tight market argument will be made in the seller's own mind regardless of what you say or do not say.

4. The Role of Threats

Threats are among the most over-used tactics in negotiation. As with the use of subtlety, ask yourself how you feel when threatened? The fact is, threats increase the likelihood that a person will respond non-rationally. And the use of threats decreases the likelihood that the type of relationship necessary for effective problem-solving and long-term trust will develop. In fact, social-psychology research indicates that using threats actually decreases the chance that you will achieve a mutually acceptable result.

While threats are often inappropriately used, research indicates that they can be effective. Whether you choose to use a threat or need to respond to a threat, your first step is to determine what makes a threat effective.

To be effective a threat must meet a number of elements. First, the threat must be heard. If the threatened party cannot hear the threat, the threat will be ineffective. This suggests that one appropriate response to a threat is simply to ignore it. Pretend you did not hear it, that it simply was not made. Another effective tactic is to call a halt, or recess to the negotiation, if it appears that a threat is likely to occur.

To be effective, a threat also must be understood as a threat. For example, a common threat is to let other people in the community know how uncooperative, demanding, or unreasonable you are. Treating this as a non-threat can be effective.

> LAWYER FOR NEWMAN: I don't think the clients of Popcheck Blank & Denis will be happy when they find out about the behavior of senior partners.

LAWYER FOR FIRM: I think our clients will be pleased to know we don't cave in to unsubstantiated charges. We have a reputation for aggressive litigation, and our clients would expect us to act consistent with that reputation.

An effective threat must also involve an issue that is valued by the person being threatened:

LAWYER FOR NEWMAN: I don't think the clients of Popcheck Blank & Denis will be happy when they find out about the behavior of senior partners.

LAWYER FOR FIRM: I think Newman should know from working at the firm that Popcheck, Blink & Denis doesn't care what other firms think. It has a reputation for aggressive behavior that might offend people. The fact that there are these unsupported charges won't make people think any less of the firm.

The threat must also be believed to be effective. Rejecting the possibility that the threat will be carried out may be effective. This may actually simply require ignoring the threat. If you are negotiating with a lawyer who threatens to sue if your client does not comply with some demand, you can usually safely ignore the threat if you know from advance preparation that this particular lawyer has not filed a lawsuit in recent history.

To be effective, a threat must also be prospective:

Lawyer 1: When other staff hear this you will....

Lawyer 2: I already have the reputation of being....

Finally, a threat must be proportionate or rational. If it is neither, ignore it.

A much different approach to dealing with threats used by problem-solvers focuses on why people make threats. Social psychologists tell us that people often make threats when they have no other tactic to use. If this is the case, the appropriate response to a threat is to provide the negotiator with an alternative approach to pursue. Take, for example, the situation where you offer a proposal, and the other person responds with, "Well, we're just going to have to sue." An appropriate response might be to get the person to focus on the more principled, systematic approach and invite them to participate:

Lawyer: That is one alternative, of course. Before you do that, let me ask you to share with me why you think my position is so unreasonable?

You might even go so far as to suggest criticism of your detailed persuasive statement.

Lawyer: That is one alternative, of course. Before you do that, let me ask you to share with me why you think my position is so unreasonable? For example, how else can we value the loss you allege your client has suffered?

C. Concessions, Reformulations, and Counter Proposals

The difficult part of making a concession is doing it and maintaining your credibility. If after making a persuasive argument you make a subsequent concession, you run the risk of losing credibility. After all, when you made your previous proposal you said that you are not going to give one more dime and now you are reaching into your pocket for another dime. The risk you run is that the concession will undercut your credibility. After your last offer you said there was no more to give and that was not true. Why should your opponent believe this time that more concessions will not be coming? The task, therefore, is to make concessions while maintaining your credibility, that is, not communicating that your last offer was pulled out of the air. If they believe that the first offer was pulled out of the air, they may believe that the new offer was also pulled out of the air and therefore wait for yet another concession. This is a particularly significant problem if you are already at your bottom line and they do not believe that you are. Deadlock is the likely result.

The principal way to make a concession while maintaining your credibility is to only make a concession that in some way is related to your prior proposal's justification. Usually this means being sure that the other side sees that you are conceding because you have been persuaded that there is something about your original justification that requires the concession.

The problem of "splitting the difference" illustrates the point. Assume our objective, detailed rationale developed previously:

Our client has authorized me to accept $330,000 to settle this case. Let me explain how we have arrived at this figure. We have done extensive research on verdicts in these types of cases. Independent of our own research we have consulted with Jury Verdict Research, Inc. I have their report here, as well as a listing of similar cases involving sexual harassment and defamation against professional women. You will see that the verdicts range between 375,000 and 1.3 million dollars. Given the public nature of this dispute and the fact that Ms. Newman is in the associate income bracket among the plaintiff's in these cases (the 1.3 million was a physician, we have a $450,000 verdict for an associate), at least a $450,000 verdict is likely. We recognize, of course, that between trial and appeals we are looking at four years to recover that amount. So we are willing to reduce it to its present value. Our accountant tells us that the present value of $450,000 in four years is $375,000. We, estimate that we will also save $45,000 in litigation expenses. Subtract that and you get $330,000.

Assume the other lawyer has countered with $200,000 and after a number of hours without movement the other lawyer says, "Why don't we just split the difference, we'll give you $265,000."

If you split this difference, what does it communicate about your original rationale? Logic would indicate that if you are now willing to move $65,000 for no reason other than it is the mid-point between two positions, the original, detailed, objective rationale was a pretext. You may not care about maintaining credibility at this point. However, if you need to be concerned about this because you, or your client, expects to deal with the other side in the future, you need to find a rationale for the move. For example, you can move from $330,000 to $265,000 and maintain credibility if the move is either explicitly or implicitly tied to one of your original reasons.

Lawyer for Newman: I have checked around, and the $330,000 makes sense based on an expected verdict of $375,000. You are asking us to essentially discount about 20 percent. Based on what, risk at trial?

Lawyer for Popcheck et al: Yes. Juries are unpredictable.

Lawyer for Newman: Well, I'll take that back to my client.

Here the lawyer has moved, but in a way that does not say the previous offer was a lie. The lawyer moves in a way that communicates the new figure is rationally based and unlikely to change.

If you follow this approach, you may find yourself in the position of wanting to concede, but being unable to because the person cannot think of a way to convince you. You may have to help the other person, as the lawyer for Newman did in the previous example, by suggesting a reason for the $65,000 concession.

Finally, even if settlement does not come immediately after an offer to split the difference, do not forget that the lawyer who made the suggestion has already indicated that the mid-point is acceptable. The practical result is that you should usually read the offer to split the difference as a unilateral concession of the suggested amount.

This same general approach should be followed by both problem-solvers as well as adversarial negotiators. A couple of differences, however, will be noted. First, because problem-solvers are trying to develop a joint solution to the problem, they typically do not refer to offers and demands. They prefer to use words and phrases such as proposal, solution, proposed solution, or "an idea to throw out on the table." Second, problem-solvers often invite the other side to critically analyze their proposal as a way of generating suggestions for improving it. Third, because the problem-solver is seeking a creative solution, they are normally less committed to a specific proposal, that is, they are more willing to reformulate an idea, and have less pride of authorship. Fourth, a problem-solver will avoid using terms such as concession and compromise, because the words denote positional bargaining. Rather, problem-solvers will "take a suggestion and reformulate a proposal."

D. Typical Exchange Tactics and a Systematic Approach

You will find in today's literature on negotiation a wide variety of negotiating tactics to become an effective negotiator. Some of these tactics we have already discussed in the context of a systematic approach to negotiation. The purpose of this text is to suggest that a systematic, principled approach will be more effective than a series of "tricks of the trade." However, many of these tactics fit well within the systematic approach presented here as examples of specific phases. Also, thinking about how these tactics fit within the systematic approach often helps you decide how to counter the tactic when it is used against you.

While a complete review of all these suggested tactics is beyond the scope of this work, a review of some of the more common suggestions is offered to support what was said earlier. There are no rules; there are only choices to make. Using any specific tactic makes sense only if it fosters the systematic approach you have chosen and is appropriate in this specific negotiation at this specific time.

1. Anger

Negotiators sometimes resort to feigned anger as a means of trying to convince an opponent that they are serious about their position. They also use it to intimidate. Real anger is the result of frustration or anxiety and is often not consciously intended to do anything.

Real anger can be quite dangerous. Anyone who loses control because of frustration and anxiety runs the risk of communicating more than he wishes. The mere act of becoming angry, if real, communicates frustration or anxiety, which itself may be important information to the other side. Also, the substance of any outburst may result in inadvertently revealing information. For example, a lawyer involved in a negotiation over the merger of two corporations might, at the prospect of deadlock, blurt out, "Your arrogance is overwhelming...." Assuming the anger is not feigned, the outburst communicates important information about how the lawyer is being perceived by the lawyer making the outburst. The lawyer subject to the outburst can choose either to foster that anger or, if she believes it is counter-productive, take steps to diffuse the anger. The outburst, for example, may reflect that a deadlock is not over the substance of the negotiation, but is the result of a clash of personalities. The lawyer subject to the outburst, therefore, might choose to try to break the deadlock by diffusing the personality clash rather then trying to make a substantive concession such as offering more money.

If you use feigned anger, be careful. The anger may induce the other person to become frustrated or anxious which, in turn, could result in the other person walking out. If anger is used against you, you may be able to take advantage of it. Listen carefully to the outburst's substance. You might try showing that you are personally hurt by the outburst. Making the other person feel guilty may help you control their anger by simply embarrassing them. In any event, your response should normally be temperate. Think twice before you respond in kind. Escalation might result in the breakdown of the negotiation and seriously interfere with the ability to start discussions later.

2. Aggression

Aggressive behavior, like anger, is designed to intimidate. As with anger, a more temperate response is usually appropriate. You might try to control the behavior by conducting the negotiation in a way that minimizes its impact. Similarly, it is harder to be aggressive with other people present, so negotiating in a team might be helpful. Likewise, it is harder to be aggressive and, of course, easier for you to terminate the meeting, if the negotiation takes place on the telephone. Negotiating at the aggressive lawyer's office might be appropriate because it makes it easier for you to terminate the session by walking out if the aggression becomes intolerable.

3. Boulwareism

Boulwareism is a tactic named after a former vice president of General Electric. The tactic involves making one offer, demand, or proposal and then never making a concession. It is really a take-it-or-leave-it tactic. The theory is that you will have gained sufficient information before making the proposal that you can communicate your best offer up front.

Looking at the tactic in light of our systematic approach, it may take considerable education on your part to convince the person you are serious. You will need to persuade the other person not only that the first offer is fair, just, and equitable, but that there is indeed no more. Most people think that a controlling principle of negotiations is that first offers are always negotiable, and you may have difficulty persuading someone that this convention does not apply.

A very real problem with this tactic is in formulating an appropriate take-it-or-leave-it offer. Negotiation is a fluid process. As you gather information, not just in formal information bargaining, but through making offers and counter-offers, as well as persuasive statements, you eventually gain the confidence to know what is truly the best proposal for you.

If you use Boulwareism you must also be prepared to stick to it. If you ever make a concession, your credibility is seriously impaired.

4. Balance or Slightly Outnumber the Other Side

Often it is suggested that you will gain an advantage in the negotiation by balancing your side's negotiators or outnumbering the other side. This may be useful. Again, going back to the systematic approach, we can see that there may be advantages. As we pointed out in Chapter 3, you cannot ignore the social-psychological dynamic of the negotiation process. Having an equal number of negotiators may make you less intimidated and therefore more effective. Likewise, outnumbering the other side may increase their anxiety.

Such tactics, however, carry a downside. If your goal is to be a cooperative problem-solver, such a tactic could destroy the relationship you are trying to achieve. Multiple negotiators, however, may be useful for other purposes. As seen from the above discussion, many competing demands are placed on a negotiator—listening, asking questions, responding to questions, and formulating proposals. Sharing these responsibilities can be a great help. Assigning a secondary negotiator the task of simply listening is useful. Periodic caucuses in which the negotiators compare notes on what has been said may give the principal negotiator a better perspective on the changing dynamic of the negotiation itself.

On the other hand, having a single negotiator has a number of advantages. A single person prevents the other side from taking advantage of potential divisions such as differences of opinion. A single negotiator places complete responsibility on one person and minimizes missteps by one negotiator interfering with the actions of a partner. A single negotiator may also find it easier to take advantage of unexpected opportunities.

A variation on the multiple negotiator is often called Mutt and Jeff or Good Cop/Bad Cop. In this situation, one negotiator appears reasonable and sympathetic while the other is demanding and aggressive. The demanding, aggressive person quickly rejects proposals and the other attempts to reach an agreement. The sympathetic negotiator then suggests concessions that might bridge the gap between his own partner and the person with whom they are negotiating. The tactic, which appears so blatantly manipulative on paper, can be used with incredible success by many negotiators and is quite popular.

5. False Demands

Demanding something the person doesn't really want is another common tactic. By communicating the false demand along with the real demands, the negotiator establishes a bargaining chip to be later traded away. Viewed in our systematic approach, a risk of this tactic is that if you are not as persuasive with this demand as all your other demands, it will be clear that it is false. In turn, you must not give it up without good reason. Finally, be prepared to face the fact that if you ask for it, you might get it.

6. First Offer

It is often said that you should never make the first offer in negotiation. As with most rules, there is an element of truth to this rule, but it is also terribly misleading. Quite often, you have no choice but to make the first offer. If, for example, you are selling something, you will normally be expected to set the asking price. While it may not be impossible to get the buyer to make the first offer, it is unusual.

Asking why a rule such as this developed is helpful in deciding its utility. In other words, what is the risk of making the first offer? Typically, the risk is that you will underestimate your position and ask for too little. The great fear in buying a house, for example, is that the seller will take your first offer and you will feel you offered too much.

Once again, thinking in terms of our systematic approach, the risk in making the first offer is that you might make it before you have sufficient information to assess the relative positions of the negotiators. The risk is not in making the first offer, but in making the first offer with insufficient information. In other words, the advantage of getting the other side to make the first offer is that they may prematurely move from the information bargaining stage into proposal stage.

As you gain information, the risk of making the first offer decreases. If you are in a situation where it appears inevitable that you will have to make the first offer, it merely emphasizes the importance of approaching the negotiation systematically; that is, to be sure to engage in adequate information bargaining before the proposal is made.

A common example of the difficulty is where a person quickly brushes off ice breaking and says, "That's great, but let's get to the point." Here is, in our framework, an attempt to get the lawyer to skip information bargaining. If the lawyer makes an offer now, there is a high risk that the lawyer will offer more than is required. The lawyer must exercise agenda control to move the process back and complete the information bargaining. For example, the lawyer might say:

> Well, I'm certainly here to see if we can do business. The fact is, though, I'll need lots of information before I can make a judgment about whether that's even possible. Why don't we do this. You've sent me some helpful information, but let me ask you some questions to clarify some things and find some

is. Finally, do not reveal to the ot[her]
be under to wrap up a deal becau[se]
to their advantage.

The above discussion should
tiation, and what occurs therein,

[CHAP]TER 8

[CRISIS AND] OUTCOME

Adversarial Approach to Exchange
• Extreme offers with limited reasons
• Threats
• Closely guarded reactions to offers
• Limited forced concessions
• Moving only for a reason
• Leaving no dollars on the table
• Using escalation
• Walking out
• Coming in with limited authority
• Using irrationality of client as leverage
• Making non-negotiable demands

[nego]tiation at which the parties either
[ma]king concessions, which might de-
[...] your side, there is no sure way to
[...]t all deals are meant to happen. In
[...] [p]arties' bargaining ranges may sim-
[...] [n]egotiation, the parties may simply
[...] acceptable to all.

[oppon]ent do not simply give-up. As with
[you]rself what is causing the problem?
[...] helps.

[Wh]ere Has Been a Failure

[be]cause a failure has occurred in one
[...] [p]rocess. Ask whether a problem ex-
[...] [t]ensions resulted in a relationship

An Integrated Approach to Excha[nge]
• Making offers that fit needs and g[oals]
• Exploring opponents offers for nee[ds]
• Making concessions based on ha[ve]
• Using probabilities of proof to mak[e]

[...] agreement? Has animosity grown
[...] [wi]ll be no agreement is that people do
[...]ve failed to develop the appropriate
[...]spent trying to foster that relation-
[...]then coming back for a fresh start,
[...] [s]ummarize the other side's case and
[...]ced to listen and to empathize with
[...] point of accurately stating it as a

The next chapter will addres[s]

[...] the information bargaining stage.
[...] [a]gree on the actual market value
[...] [of] reaching agreement. Is there a
[...] rate? Perhaps you have not been
[...]ent made irrational concessions, at-
[...]aps, and therefore been unable to

persuade each other that you are indeed at your bottom line? Stopping to assess the negotiation in terms of the stages may help you respond to the impending deadlock, or prevent it entirely.

2. Consider Changing Strategy

If you are an adversarial negotiator, as deadlock approaches you should probably consider a fundamental change in strategy. Remember from Chapter 1 that what makes problem-solving particularly effective is trust or little risk. Has trust developed, or is there no risk, so that you can move to problem-solving? Or, if deadlock is near and you really need to reach an agreement, ask yourself if you will lose anything by abandoning your position, expressing your needs, interests, and desires, and seeking a problem-solving solution. Of course, you will not always overcome the deadlock, but you have little to lose at this point by focusing the discussion on underlying needs.

3. Third Party Intervention: Alternate Dispute Resolution

In certain circumstances, you may avoid deadlock by involving third parties such as mediators. Where the negotiation involves a dispute between the parties, and negotiation does not appear to be able to settle the dispute, you might consider some form of alternate dispute resolution. Use of alternate dispute resolution may be particularly appropriate where the dispute can escalate into an expensive, time consuming, emotionally draining lawsuit.

A complete discussion of the various forms of alternate dispute resolution is beyond the scope of this book, however, it may be useful to have a basic understanding of what various options are available. Typically, privately arranged alternate dispute resolution includes negotiation as well as:

❖ arbitration, both binding and non-binding;

❖ mediation;

❖ summary jury trials/mini-trials;

❖ a combination of some or all of the above.

These types of third party intervention may be effective because each helps to:

❖ reduce irrationality;

❖ reduce impact of social-psychological influences;

- ❖ explore alternative solutions;

- ❖ provide opportunities for graceful retreat; and

- ❖ facilitate communication.

a. Arbitration

Arbitration is typically viewed as an alternative to litigation. In essence, arbitration is a private form of litigation in which the parties choose the person who, after hearing some form of presentation from each side of the dispute, renders a decision much as a judge would. The theory is that a neutral third party in a private setting has several advantages, including:

- ❖ the parties can select an arbitrator that has particular experience with the type of issues raised in the dispute;

- ❖ the dispute can be resolved privately, thus avoiding much of the adverse publicity associated with a public lawsuit;

- ❖ the arbitration tends to be more informal, and it is even possible for the parties to represent themselves rather than hire an attorney;

- ❖ arbitration can be completed more quickly than a lawsuit;

- ❖ arbitration may save money.

Arbitration is based on an agreement of the parties. As such, the parties can tailor the arbitration based on the particular needs of the dispute. A primary point of agreement will have to be whether the arbitration will be binding or non-binding. The parties can agree that the arbitrator's decision is binding and hence enforceable against the losing party. On the other hand, they can agree that the result is non-binding. If the decision is non-binding, the result is in effect advisory and, hence, may suggest to the losing party that they should not pursue the matter through litigation because they will probably lose.

b. Mediation

Mediation is the process by which a neutral third party assists the parties to the dispute in resolving the matter. A mediator has no authority to impose a solution and often does not even propose solutions, but rather assists the parties to come to their own agreement. Because the parties normally must agree to mediation, as with arbitration you can tailor the precise role of the mediator to a specific problem. More will be said about how to think strategically about using a mediator in Chapter 9.

c. Summary Jury Trials/Mini Trials

As a variation on a form of arbitration, trials by private judges are becoming more popular. The precise name given to these private trials varies depending on the particular ground rules established, but in general, each method relies upon a private judge to conduct a form of trial. The trial is often an abbreviated version of what would happen in court. The abbreviations might consist of presenting testimony in summary form, or in limiting the time available to each side to present evidence. A particularly creative variation is to conduct such a mini-trial and, rather than having the judge make a decision, the disputants return to the negotiation table to see if they can settle the dispute with their new awareness of how the trial might go.

B. The Outcome

Every negotiation is unique when it comes to the specifics of what makes a good outcome. There are, however, a number of general considerations to keep in mind. The outcome should, in no particular order:

❖ reflect the parties' goals and authority;

❖ create a minimum of new problems;

❖ be efficient;

❖ be achievable;

❖ be enforceable;

❖ be implementable;

❖ be fair, just, and equitable;

❖ have the desired level of specificity/ambiguity;

❖ be comprehensive;

❖ anticipate contingencies.

C. Wrap-up

The negotiation as a whole, and individual sessions of a negotiation, must be ended just as they must begin. Parties often forget that ending entails a number of concerns. First, just as you want to start the negotiation setting the proper tone, you want to end it with the appropriate tone. People tend to remember most what they hear first and last, so the ending should involve rapport building (or perhaps rebuilding).

On a substantive level the wrap-up should include a summary of the work completed to that point and, if the negotiation is complete, you should completely restate the agreement reached. If additional negotiation is required, you should summarize progress to date so that there will be less chance of misinterpretation at the next session.

At the end of each session, each party should have a clear understanding of what their next step will be and when the next meeting (or how it will be determined) will take place. If the other person has indicated during the negotiation that she will provide you with certain financial information, for example, you must reiterate that promise and establish a specific time frame. If you have promised to do something, restate that commitment and time frame.

D. Memorialization

In today's world, almost any negotiation, especially one involving lawyers, will end with some form of writing that is a contract or summary of the negotiation. Given the free flowing nature of negotiation and the limitations of the human mind, when someone sits down to summarize the agreement often certain issues will remain unresolved, or at least their resolution is ambiguous. Given this circumstance, it makes sense that you should do the summary yourself, if possible. This allows you the first opportunity to resolve these issues or ambiguities. Presenting your resolution to the other side is, in a sense, establishing the agenda for resolution of these hopefully minor issues.

The final writeup can lead to an unwinding of the deal. In some situations, then, lawyers can again learn from the international arena. President Jimmy Carter, for example, feels that the parties should be always looking towards drafting one agreement. The international mediator can present a single document back and forth between the parties until the parties have agreed in writing on the terms of the deal. The lesson for lawyers may be for the lawyers to leave the writeup of the agreement for the mediator to draft and present to each party.

Adversarial Approach to Deadlock	Problem-Solver Approach to Deadlock
• Appear to make best final offer • Use escalation • Walk out • Refuse further discussion and make it difficult to communicate	• Verify deadlock and restate last positions • Examine positions for psychological biases • Bargain hypothetically, without any commitments • Propose discussion of ways to persuade opponent's client to move • Propose discussion of ways to persuade your client to move • Brainstorm what might make a difference • Try to get on the same board or page • Raise alternative means to verify, evaluate, and develop processes of trust • Consolidate gains and reduce differences • Use ethical understanding to defuse anger • Revisit underlying needs and goals • Suggest arbitration or mediation

Integrated Approach
• Moves from adversarial to problem-solving depending on trust and ripeness

CHAPTER 9
NEGOTIATORS AND MEDIATORS

One of the most important lessons that negotiation theory and practice teach today's lawyers is how to think strategically about mediation. That is because mediators fall into two different types. Most are retired judges who are using their credibility gained in helping resolve other cases in court to aid the parties' valuation of their cases. In this type of mediation, the mediators are willing to provide an objective perspective to help the parties evaluate their strengths and weaknesses. Others see themselves as neutrals. They eschew giving opinions regarding a case's value as unethical. They merely seek to facilitate communication, understanding, and empathy between the disputants, and then help them problem-solve by generating creative options for a solution. These mediators help the parties predict consequences, and set up monitoring devices to ensure the solutions are carried out.

For example, lawyers can learn lessons from Sadat's insertion of "mediator" President Jimmy Carter to help it make peace with Israel. Sadat initiated conversations with Carter, pledged his cooperation, and enlisted his support in picking the timing, place, and parties. Note that President Carter, with an understanding that he did not want the UN Security Council members, including Russia and China, to be at the table, invited only Israel and Egypt to Camp David. Would Egypt (and President Carter) eventually sell out the Palestinians in order to secure peace with Israel? That is a question for history. Our point here is that a mediator can have his own agenda, interest, and priorities. And if a mediator weighs in with his own values, he can shape the outcome in significant ways.

There are as many different pre-mediation processes and mediation stages as there are mediators. Some mediators are very informal and demand very little in the way of a pre-mediation production of discovery and documents. Others are more formal, and demand the signing of a pre-mediation agreement in which the parties agree to mediate in good faith, provide full and complete answers to the mediator about the strengths and weaknesses in their cases, and agree not to fail to disclose material facts that relate to the fair resolution of the dispute.

147

One of the most important factors in choosing a mediator is the mediator's reputation of being prepared and invested in the process. Over and over again at the Camp David Twenty-Fifth Anniversary Forum, the parties involved commented that President Carter's level of detailed preparation was key to the success of the negotiations. Carter reportedly had briefing books that included minute details, so that he even knew what time of day was best to approach each party with proposals, based on an investigation of the parties' personal work habits. Such detailed preparation allowed President Carter to adapt strategy and tactics, to go from group meetings, to caucuses, to taking breaks, to taking walks, to shuttling back and forth, with proposals and suggestions, which kept the negotiation alive, even when the outlook was bleak.

As to the stages of mediation, some follow the stages of a hearing, with the parties giving an opening statement, followed by the asking of questions of each other, and then fact investigation conducted by the mediator. There are some extreme types of position bargaining mediation that do away with opening statements. Worrying that opening statements just make parties more wed to their side of the case, these mediators prefer to demand that the parties start by making opening offers and then concessions in order to move the parties to a solution. Using "split the difference" strategies, probabilities, risk analysis, discounting to present value concepts, and economic analysis, these mediators try to bring the parties into agreement about the dollar value of their case.

There are some who will make extensive use of caucuses between mediator and each side; some with lawyers present, some with lawyers and clients, some with just clients present. During these caucuses some mediators use confidentiality to promote an understanding of how far apart each side is, and, if there are significant differences in how each side sees the case, the mediator might try to persuade the parties where they are being unrealistic. Some then will engage in "shuttle" diplomacy between the parties until the matter is resolved.

Other mediators resist valuing the case. If there is deadlock, these mediators prefer to bring the parties together to facilitate the exchange of creative problem-solving solutions through brainstorming and careful examination and exploration of each side's underlying goals and needs.

A. An Integrated Approach to Preparing for Mediation

Preparation for mediation is informed by the same stages of preparation that should be studied for any negotiation: the lawyer should consider issues of:

(Assessment)

Preparation and planning including

Style and strategy (Will the lawyer be a competitive adversarial, a cooperative adversarial, a cooperative problem-solver, a cooperative adversarial?)

Ice breaking (Will the lawyer be friendly and engage in rapport building with the mediator, the opposing lawyer, or the opposing client? What information might be gained in this time of informality? Should an apology be offered, or empathy expressed as a matter of setting the right tone?)

Agenda control (Will the lawyer suggest an agenda to the mediator during the opening, or during the first caucus? Will the lawyer suggest a process for information exchange to the mediator that might be suggested to the opposing party(ies)? Will the lawyer suggest a problem-solving process for the mediation, seeking to identify shared needs, independent needs, and needs in conflict, and then engage in a suggestion of creative win/win solutions for resolving the dispute?)

(Exchange and Assessment)

Information bargaining (What questions do you need answered before you are willing to trust the other side with vital information? Will you block information exchange until you are satisfied that the other side is bargaining in good faith? How will you answer the mediator's attempts to determine your bottom line? Will you engage in a pre-mediation counseling with the client, to teach the client to reveal the client's authority in stages, based on what you learn for the opposition? How will you prepare the client to answer the question, what is the most (least) you are willing to give to the other side?)

Proposals, offers, demands (What will be your opening offer? What persuasive reasons will you give to justify your position?)

Persuasion/Justification (Will you be prepared to make an opening/closing with all the care that you would if you were giving it to a jury? Will you use exhibits and display technology to give the mediator and opponent a view of what the factfinder will be shown at trial? Even in cases where the mediator has done away with opening statements, will you give a disk, hard copy of exhibits, or other written statement of your case to the mediator and opponent?)

(Assessment, Exchange, Persuasion)

Concessions/Reformulation (What concessions will you make and when will you make them? Will you be prepared to give reasons for your concessions, or credit the opponent for having persuaded you to make the concession? Will you be cooperative or competitive during the concession phase?)

Crisis: resolution or deadlock (Will you walk away? Engage in brainstorming? Propose creative solutions? Agree to a process for future mediation?)

Closing or Wrap-up (Will you engage in a restatement of the final solution before agreement?)

Memorialization or Write-up (What enforceability concerns does the solution raise, and what contingencies need to be put in place to both verify what has been stated and exchanged, and to implement the agreement as intended? Will you suggest that the mediator do the wrap-up and control the write up?)

B. Particular Position Bargaining Considerations for Mediation

Mediators provide a number of useful purposes when seen in light of a position bargaining strategy.

❖ The mediator can lend credibility to the client's valuation of the case

❖ The mediator can help the parties get information about the opponent's bottom line, strengths, and weaknesses in their case

❖ The mediator can act as an expert evaluator of the case in light of the experience in judging responsibility or evaluating credibility and persuasiveness of stories, and in light of their substantive/technical expertise

❖ The mediator can use position bargaining strategies to move the parties to a reasoned settlement

❖ The mediator can suggest use of deadlines

The mediator can help you:

❖ Probe positions and test them for evidence

❖ Use contracts and processes for exchange of information

❖ Use confidentiality and caucuses to "leak" information to each side

❖ Use persuasion

❖ Use trading concessions of equal value

❖ Splitting the difference

C. Particular Problem-Solving Considerations for Mediation

As we have discussed, some mediators, thought of as neutrals or facilitators, eschew valuation and position bargaining strategies when they conduct mediations. Facilitative mediators are particularly good for implementation of a problem-solving strategy for resolving the dispute. If the mediator will use techniques to maintain neutrality, refuse case evaluation, facilitate communication, and use brainstorming and other counseling techniques to create win/win solutions, then the mediator can be vital to the implementation of a problem-solving strategy.

The problem-solving mediator can:

❖ Suggest problem-solving processes

❖ Overcome opponent resistance to problem-solving strategies by making suggestions from the position of neutrality. Where these same solutions suggested by a lawyer negotiator might be rejected, because they are distrusted and viewed as tricks and manipulations, when offered by a neutral they will more likely be adopted.

❖ Facilitate discussion of underlying goals and values

❖ Create fair processes for providing information and valuation

❖ Facilitate the generation of multiple alternative solutions that create win/win outcomes

❖ Suggest creative valuation methods to provide means for parties to turn values into positions

❖ Create implementation processes that build in fairness, predictability, and trust

Notice how differently you should prepare for a problem-solving mediation.

❖ Your audience of your persuasion is the opposing side, not the mediator.

❖ Your language is that of a problem-solver. You talk of goals and needs, not positions or interest.

But beware. If your opponent employs a classic position bargaining strategy, it is unlikely that he or she will think to come armed with the information to engage in broader problem-solving. Even if the parties tried to implement a problem-solving strategy in the negotiation, without buy in up front, the early sessions are likely to be unproductive until the bargainer is prepared with a broader understanding of the client's goals, or, in the worst case, until the bargainer feigns interest in problem-solving, only to discover weaknesses in your case.

Suggesting a facilitative mediator creates a different incentive. Parties will likely be required to be present. The mediator can ask critical questions of each side, and brainstorm for various alternatives. Other broader business concerns might be explored, and agreements might be reached which help the parties work together fairly to promote each side's legitimate interests. During mediation, adequate apologies can take place. Parties can better judge the sincerity of the apology. They can better protect against attribution error. (See Chapter 3).

Mediators are also particularly useful to the parties in both intractable disputes and in multi-party disputes.

When, then, should lawyers counsel their clients to consider the advantages of mediation? And how should the lawyer think strategically about mediation in order to implement the client's goals?

Problem 9.1
Application to *Green v. Hall and Rose*

In order to understand this point the lawyer must think about how a mediator might facilitate a different kind of resolution of the dispute between the Greens in their dispute with their realtor and the homeowner. Remember the Greens, who are African American, were assured by their realtor that their bid would be accepted, and were not given a chance to raise their offer by the homeowner, who accepted the offer of a white buyer instead of the Greens. Often, the case is not resolved, and the parties end up going to court, though no one wants this. In the alternative, the Green's are paid close to $60,000, but only after Hall and Rose are cajoled into ponying up more money. Before a mediator evaluator, the case often resolves at about the same point. Before a neutral mediator, who focuses on broader client goals and objectives, the chance at some more creative and jointly beneficial solution may be improved.

If the lawyer understands how and why a mediator might facilitate such a better, tailored outcome, it might lead the lawyer to recommend, and the client to choose, mediation.

For example, the Greens might have the following, somewhat conflicting goals and objectives stated as follows:

—The Greens want an injunction to prevent future discrimination

—The Greens want any damages to compensate for the loss of their bargain

—The Greens want damages to deter the realtor and homeowner from subjecting other African Americans to the treatment they received

—The Greens want a public apology from both of the parties

D. When to Mediate: Intractable Conflicts and Multi-Party Disputes

In the business context in particular, where clients may more readily think in terms of transactions rather than disputes, these mediator-facilitated problem-solving solutions often work to the overall betterment of both sides. In litigation, the parties often resolve their disputes unassisted. Yet, other times, the parties are not able to negotiate unassisted to an agreement. Perhaps there is bad blood between the clients, or their lawyers, or there is too much at stake, or it is a matter of principal. Perhaps the size or complexity of the dispute prevents any approach other than a traditional litigation approach.

Peter Coleman, Director of the International Center for Cooperation and Conflict Resolution, in an article on intractable conflicts in the international arena, sheds light on the intractability of conflicts in traditional litigation. His first factor of intractability is the *time and intensity* of the conflict. It is interesting to note how the standard litigation processes of complaint and answer, and interrogatories and depositions add time and intensity to the dispute between the parties and certainly to their lawyers. Mediation prefiling is a strategy that parties should employ if they want to avoid intensifying the dispute.

The second factor is *issue centrality*: that the conflict involves needs or values that are critical to the disputants' survival. Disputes over the purchase of a home that is denied on the basis of racism, spousal and child support payments, medical costs, or disputes that result in a company going out of business might be of this type. Disputes with insurance companies shouldn't be of this type, as one tenet of insurance is to pass on the costs in future premiums they charge to the client or other customers.

Third is *conflict pervasiveness*: that the conflict affects the disputants in their everyday life and work.

Next, is a feeling the parties share. That feeling is a feeling of *hopelessness*.

Fifth, parties are *motivated to harm* the other side. In the litigation process, the parties have sought Rule 11 sanctions, made ethics complaints to the bar about the lawyers, and have stated intentions to "destroy," "put out of business," and "make sure that this never happens again." Finally, the parties have repeatedly *resisted efforts to resolve* the dispute, but nothing seems to have worked.

In the above situations, the lawyer is wise to consider whether a mediator ought to be employed. The lawyer most often sees the need for mediation where they have been involved in protracted and heated negotiations, with no movement between the parties.[17]

E. Social Science Teachings about Mediation

If a lawyer knows what social science literature suggests about how mediators might help resolve even intractable conflicts, then the lawyers might prepare themselves and their clients to be ready to fit into these processes.[18] Litigators should know about this literature as it provides guidance to the ways that mediators are likely to see the process. As a result, it can help the litigator plan when to mediate, how the mediation will likely be conducted, and what processes the mediator might use to help the parties reach resolution.

Peter Coleman suggests a number of guidelines that should be employed by mediators to try and overcome the resistance the parties have to settlement of even intractable conflicts. His guidelines are directed to intervenors or mediators. When the lawyer determines that either the lawyer him or her self, or the opposing side, is unwilling to employ these guidelines by themselves then a mediator can provide the missing ingredient. These guidelines are:

Guideline 1: Conduct a thorough analysis of the conflict system (its history, context, issues, and dynamics) prior to intervention.

Mediators can design a presentation process in the hearing of the concerned parties to make sure each side gets a chance to be heard, and be assured that the mediator understands the perspective of each party. (Remember that Rusk's listening for understanding model is particularly good for fulfilling this guideline. See Chapter 3.)

Guideline 2: Initial concern for the mediator should be to establish or foster an authentic experience of "ripeness" among the disputants or among the key representatives of each of the groups.

---

17 Peter T. Coleman and Morton Deutsch, The Handbook of Conflict Resolution, Theory and Practice, Chapter 21, pp. 429–439, (2000).

18 Peter T. Coleman, *Intractable Conflict*, Morton Duetsch & Peter T. Coleman, eds. The Handbook of Dispute Resolution: Theory and Practice, 428, (2002).

Lawyers can create this sense of ripeness by picking a skilled and fair mediator who has been successful in other difficult disputes, and helping create a just and particularized solution to the dispute that lasts. The reputation of the mediator can create a sense of "ripeness" among the parties that now is the time to get this settled. One variable that can help the lawyer in suggesting the timing of the mediation can be whether there has been a recent or near catastrophe. In addition, if the cost of stalemate has been recalculated and is now projected to raise unacceptable costs to both sides (for example, the likely number of plaintiffs in the future class will make it such that the existing plaintiffs will not receive fair compensation), then the time is ripe for mediation.

Guideline 3: Initially, the mediator should orient the disputants toward the primary objective of defining a fair, constructive process of conflict engagement, and away from the objectives of achieving outcomes that resolve the conflict.

The 9/11 commission experience is instructive here. Before resolving the conflict the parties should focus on a fair process. This required input from the harmed and flexibility from the mediator to hear the objections, and help design a process that would be fair. Again, a skilled mediator is vital to this occurring, but lawyers can "feed" the mediator suggestions regarding a fair process that will live within the limits of the client's goals and objectives.

Guideline 4: Given the complexity of intractable conflict, analysis and intervention must be embedded in a multidisciplinary framework.

Where a lawyer understands the social, psychological, economic, and justice implications involved in an intractable dispute, he can best prepare a process that will satisfy the parties. For example, where there are multiple parties and multiple interests, in a mass tort setting, democratic theories require that each party has representation and a voice in the design of the process. In addition, any economic analysis must be designed to insure a reliable process of valuing individual harms. Document retrievals and language searches should be implemented that will insure fairness. Experts need to be drawn from different disciplines to advise and balance different biases within fields. The process needs to be open. The steps in each decision must to be clearly articulated. Panels of decision makers must be accountable for their decisions. While mediators can design these, the lawyers and their clients can suggest a structure that works and lasts.

Guideline 5: Elicitive approaches to conflict intervention, particularly when working across cultures, tend to be more respectful of disputants, more empowering and sustainable, and generally more effective than prescriptive approaches.

The problem-solvers and facilitative neutral mediators are cheering! If the disputants can suggest the solution, they are more likely to own it and abide by it than if it is forced on them by, for example, Congress (in the case of 9/11), or by the U.S. (in the case of Iraq). What is true on a national or international scale is true in private litigation. If the disputants can suggest, have input, and seem to have selected the process, they are more likely to live by it. (Again, the litigator might suggest that the mediator propose a solution to the other disputants and make it seem as if it were their own demand to which the litigant is "forced" to accede.)

Guideline 6: Short term (crisis management) interventions need to be coordinated and mindful of long term objectives and interventions.

This guideline is for the mediator, but it is the job of the advocate to remind the mediator of the long term goals of their client in mediation and insure that these are not harmed.

Guideline 7: When working with conflicts between large groups (such as ethnic groups and communities), it is useful to concentrate interventions on the "midlevel" leadership representing each group.

Coleman writes about this guideline in the context of international disputes:

> The work of John Burton, Herbert Kelman, John Paul Lederach, and others has emphasized targeting for intervention with certain types of leaders with groups and communities engaged in protracted social conflicts. These leaders, labeled "track II diplomats" or "middle-range leaders," are typically influential, unofficial representatives (members of the media; former or potential government officials; leaders of busi-

157

ness, educational, religious, union, and other local institutions) from opposing sides of a conflict who represent the mainstream of each community and reflect the attitudes and interests of their respective communities.

There are several advantages to working with such midlevel representatives. It is efficient because midlevel representatives have influence going up and down the ladder. Midlevel representatives are more realistic because these have seen the good and bad in the parties they represent. They are also not usually constrained by their roles to take the more extreme positions.

Guideline 8: The general intervention strategy must integrate appropriate approaches for issues rooted in the past, the present, and the future.

Mediators mediating the mass multi-party dispute are worried that any short-term solution will be short term and leave future claimants without a remedy. Again, the litigator should prepare for the mediation and be ready to show why the resolution is designed to last.

F. Conclusion

In determining how to think strategically about mediation, the lawyer must first determine what kind of mediator he wants to mediate the session. If the mediator is a retired judge or evaluative mediator, the lawyer should consider the following strategies:

❖ Forming an implied alliance with the mediator by making a concession that will communicate your good faith, your reasonableness, and your willingness to settle

❖ Using a concession pattern that communicates that your first offer was close to your bottom line

❖ Enlisting the mediator to help you discover the weaknesses of the opposing side's case

❖ Use cooperative blocking techniques, i.e., over answering questions, setting up trades for information, and staggering offers in a way to insure the good faith of the opposition

❖ If the client is present, explain to the client the importance of information exchange and the ability of the client to let the lawyer communicate the client's positions

❖ If the client is present, teach the client how to block the mediator's questions, or to answer, but on the condition of confidentiality

If the mediator is a neutral facilitator, the lawyer should consider the following strategies:

❖ Communicating with the mediator in terms of the client's needs and goals

❖ Request that the mediator ask for information from the other side to insure that they are mediating in good faith

❖ Identify Shared Needs, Independent Needs, and Conflicting Needs

❖ Enlist the mediator in presenting creative solutions, as if they came from the mediator. (This will enhance the solutions acceptability, when it is seen as coming from the neutral.)

In order for a litigator to think strategically about implementing the client's goals and objectives, the litigator needs to understand theory choices and strategies that are likely to come into play. The two prominent strategies are position bargaining, or adversarial bargaining, and problem-solving. Position bargaining is the most common strategy employed by bargainers and involves taking positions to learn how your opponent likely sees his case and determining how to move the opposition into a solution that meets your client's goals. Problem-solving, on other hand, involves creating a relationship between the parties of trust and cooperation so that a better and more creative solution can be devised. Problem-solving strategies often require the involvement of a mediator for the promise of problem-solving to be fully implemented.

Understanding these strategy choices can help you better counsel the client about the means by which his goals might be achieved. The strategies can also be useful for helping both client and lawyer understand the strengths, weaknesses, and risks involved in resolving their case, and finally, help the client make the best strategic moves to implement his goals.

Evaluative Mediator	Facilitative Neutral or Transformative Mediator
• Written submissions of facts and issues • May not ask for opening statement at session • Asks to go into caucus with each side • Asks for opening offer • Expresses opinion on offer and tries to suggest where offer overstates position • Tests proof of facts with confidentiality • Expresses opinion on chances of success at trial • Tries to generate concessions and more realistic bottom line • Does same with other side • Shuttle diplomacy till agreement • If deadlock, uses persuasion on side out of line in evaluator's opinion	• Written commitment pre-session to cooperate and disclose and negotiate in good faith • Asks each side to describe their perspectives • Each side addresses other side, not the mediator, during their opening statement • Advocate should use the language of goals and needs, not offers and positions • Caucus used to ask for sensitive information and to ask about party's empathy for other side (How do you think the other side will react to your proposal? What should I use to convince them to understand our goals?) • Ask what is fair, in addition to what they want • Seeks to establish ethical understanding of each side • Seeks out and diffuses attribution and bias errors • Joint session asks parties what solutions they see • Brainstorm additional solutions • Facilitate party discussion underlying needs and goals • Asks parties to determine solutions • Where there is deadlock, suggest party processes for breaking deadlock that are objectively verifiable and fair • No evaluation given • Facilitates discussion of solutions for societal fairness • Sets up monitoring devices

Integrated Approach to Mediation
• A mediation process designed for the particular dispute and particular disputants
• Written submissions of facts and issues
• Written commitment up front to cooperate and disclose and negotiate in good faith
• May not ask for opening statement at session if determines parties will not benefit but will become more intransient from making opening statement
• May ask each side to describe their perspectives to facilitate empathy
• Asks parties to describe broader goals and shared needs
• Asks to go into caucus with each side
• Refuses caucuses to promote trust and communication
• Or caucus used to ask for sensitive information and to ask about party's empathy for other side
• Tests proof of facts with confidentiality offer either in joint session or in caucus
• Asks parties to brainstorm possible solutions
• Facilitates conversation between the parties to develop understanding of economic, social, and psychological consequences
• Asks for opening offer
• Asks permission to express opinion on offer and to suggest where offer overstates position
• Asks permission, (Would it be helpful if I told you....) expresses opinion on chances of success at trial
• Tries to generate concessions and more realistic bottom line
• Does same with other side
• Shuttle diplomacy till agreement
• If deadlock, uses persuasion on side out of line (in mediator's opinion)
• Seeks to establish ethical understanding of each side
• Seeks out and diffuses attribution and bias errors
• Joint session asks parties what solutions they see
• Brainstorm additional solutions
• Facilitate party discussion underlying needs and goals
• Asks parties to determine solutions
• Where there is deadlock, suggest party processes for breaking deadlock that are objectively verifiable and fair
• No evaluation given or upon request suggest evaluation
• Facilitates discussion of solutions for societal fairness
• Sets up monitoring devices

CHAPTER 10
MULTI-PARTY NEGOTIATIONS

Up to this point, except for a brief foray during our discussion of mediation, our focus has been on two-party negotiations. As we have seen, there are a number of significant barriers to negotiated settlement of a two-party dispute. There are biasing errors for each side to deal with. There are failures in trust and information exchange. There are game theory reasons why a particular party might want to withhold and conceal information to obtain a bargaining advantage. As a result, there are negotiation failures even when there are solutions that would provide an efficient, fair, and lasting resolution to a dispute.

As difficult as these barriers are in a two-party dispute, they become even more complex in a multi-party dispute. This is particularly true because even though some parties want to settle, others can gain advantages through **holding out** and **opting out** from the final agreement. These strategies threaten finality and place the fair resolution of a dispute into jeopardy. Consensus resolution is often unworkable, and so parties agree to resolve matters by majority voting, or with reference to agreements by a "sufficient consensus" of the disputants. Some argue that where there is a "sufficient consensus," the "winners" can negotiate side agreements with the hold outs, and every one will reach resolution. In the end then, the resolution of multi-party disputes will likely be negotiated between two parties; the winners, or a sufficient consensus of winners, and the hold outs.

While there are different strategic considerations that arise with multiple party negotiations, the same two strategic frameworks inform those choices, and an integrative approach—one that blends adversarial and problem-solving strategies can help you prepare for multi-party negotiations.

A. Criminal Context

Consider what happens when two alleged co-conspirators plea bargain with the state. If the negotiation starts in the interrogation stage, the state is looking to form an alliance with one of the defendants to get information about the two of them. If one of the defendants is your client, and can get a deal that is better than if the state gets the co-operation of the other co-conspirator against your client, it makes sense to accept the deal. If, however, the state's case against both defendants will fail if each fails to cooperate with the state, then it makes better sense for the defendants to reach a joint defense agreement, and for your client to refuse to deal with the police. The "prisoner's" dilemma is that during the interrogation stage, they don't know whether the other is cooperating, and whether the alleged co-conspirator sees the same likely success of a joint defense agreement.

The case turns on the strategic control of information—both what each defendant gives and what the defendant can get from the state. You try to find out from the state what information they have and the likelihood that they will be able to either get the co-conspirator's coop-eration, or will be able to prove their case independent of your client's cooperation.

Traditional strategy by the lawyer bargainer is to get the maxi-mum from his own client about what the state knows. The bargainer then tries to get the most from the state about what it knows and seeks to be a risk calculation predicting whether his client will do better by forming an alliance. The bargainer wants to go into the session with a clear understanding of his client's bottom line (understanding of what is the worst result they will take) and by taking positions against the prosecutor to determine what the prosecutor has, and whether reaching a deal with the prosecutor is the best way to insure the client's bottom line.

The same basic calculations hold in a civil case, for both position-bargaining plaintiffs and defendants. Where there are multiple plain-tiffs, the plaintiffs may want to cooperate with each other if they can do better with an average recovery (block information about the par-ticular weaknesses and contributory negligence or assumption of risk of their client) by reaching a deal with each other to cooperate against the defendant.

Where there is a single plaintiff, like a prosecutor, the plaintiff seeks to get total maximum recovery by determining whether they can best get this by reaching an alliance with one of the defendants (Mary Carter agreements). The defendants also are trying to determine whether it is better to reach a joint defense agreement, or to reach an individual agreement with the plaintiff.

B. Mass Torts

Ford Bronco and Firestone tire cases demonstrate the complexities where the defendants not only are trying to calculate how they will fare against an uncertain size class of plaintiffs, but also figure in the costs of their negotiations with government and any recall the government might order. As to any one defendant, the calculation depends on determining:

❖ The number of potential claimants

❖ The average size of their damages

❖ The setoffs for plaintiff's own behavior

❖ The chances of success of the average case

❖ The affect on the size of future claimants of settling with existing claimants

❖ The cost of recall

Alliances or coalitions can be formed to better assess the information needed to make the calculation. In addition, different procedures need to be considered for getting information to assess the risks and values of the claims. So the defendant might consider:

❖ Trying a sampling of representative cases in order to get better information to assess the number, size of damages, and setoffs

❖ Using class actions (for settlement purposes) as a vehicle for getting information about the number of claimants and classes of claimants

❖ Using Multidistrict Litigation (MDL) to get information through res judicata principles about causation, the ability of an expert to use certain kinds of expert testimony, and whether any defenses might bar all suits, or certain classes of suits

❖ Using bankruptcy law to classify claimants, and determine average recoveries, get rid of punitive damages claims, and/or preserve key business assets through Chapter 11 bankruptcy, in order to sanitize the business from claims and avoid payments to unknown, future claimants.

C. Bankruptcy as Forum for Dispute Resolution

One of the common misperceptions that a client has is that bankruptcy is not an option when thinking about dispute resolution. This is because there are a number of myths about bankruptcy that need to be looked at carefully:

❖ *Myth 1. The corporate board may have obligations to equity holders and option holders, that are likely lost when bankruptcy is declared.*

At some point, because the fiduciary obligation runs to the corporation and not just to the equity holders, the board's obligations do run to the creditor. This may give the management the cover to protect key business assets from certain classes of claimants. As a result, management survives for a another day, protecting their own employment and future income. In fact, in a mass tort situation, where there is ongoing liability, the existing claimants and creditors may have a conflict of interest with future claimants. They might join with management and not contest bankruptcy or bankruptcy plans, if they determine it is better for their existing claimants and themselves to get a fee certain now, and wash the debtor clean of future claims against it in its reformed state.

❖ *Myth 2. Bankruptcy hurts relationships with suppliers, creditors, and customers effecting the ongoing nature of the business.*

Empirical studies on the effects of bankruptcy on the surviving business do not bear this out, at least not with the big players. Filing bankruptcy did not hurt United, or USAir, or Federal Mogul, in its ongoing relationships with suppliers, creditors and customers, at least not as it effected their ability to secure the necessary supplies, credit, or maintain its customer base, during the term of the bankruptcy proceeding.

❖ *Myth 3. Bankruptcy litigation costs—each party or group of parties gets an attorney and their costs get paid before other business costs to the detriment of the ongoing business.*

❖ *Myth 4. When in bankruptcy, the business can only conduct normal business, and mergers and acquisitions are outlawed. Other unusual business actions must be passed before committees. The business is less nimble and can't respond quickly enough in the market.*

❖ *Myth 5. Bankruptcy requires insolvency.*

Note that some commentators think that the constitution requires a finding of insolvency.[19] Bankruptcy legislation and bankruptcy practice suggests otherwise. Others are less sure, and the practice seems to be to the contrary.[20]

Advantages of the bankruptcy system that must be considered are:

❖ Bankruptcy may allow you to protect your key assets and scrub them from future liability

❖ Individual bankruptcy decisions are non-reviewable

❖ Punitive damages may disappear (though fraud and intentional torts are not supposed to disappear in bankruptcy)

D. Coalitions and Alliances

Setting aside for the moment the mass tort situation, the conventional multi-party lawsuit seems to be simply a matter of controlling information, using position bargaining techniques to control the opposition's view of the case, and maximizing the client's return. Alliances and agreements to cooperate should be used to control information and used to maximize return and minimize harm.

Yet there are a number of social and psychological affects from alliances and coalitions that need to be examined.

---

19 Thomas E. Plank, *The Constitutional Limitations of Bankruptcy*, 63 TENN.L.REV. 487, 565 (1996).

20 George Kuney, *Bankruptcy & Recovery of Lost Damages*, 71 TENN.L.REV. 81 (2003).

First, there is a tendency for some coalitions, or "enclaves" of simi-larly-situated decision makers, to polarize, or take extreme positions. For example, institutional defendants, like tobacco companies and fami-lies of persons who died from smoking, might meet and agree to share information, and gradually become more extreme in the positions they take. They may tend to demonize the opposition and miss the legitimacy of the competing claims.

Second, coalitions can sow mistrust. Our experience observing three-party negotiations, where parties are permitted to form alliances, bears witness to the strong psychological affects that pre-negotiation coalitions have on causing mistrust and deadlock, even when the clients have given their lawyers plenty of authority to settle the case.

The problem-solver would predict as much. Position bargainers who stonewall will not engender a communication process that will lead to a fair resolution of the dispute. Not only will the parties be highly skeptical of the information they get from the other side, they will likely attribute wrongful intent on both parties, raising the stakes on both sides of the table. In addition, position bargaining will more often lead to making deals with the wrong party, with the result that parties lose at trial.

It is better, say the problem-solvers, to design a negotiation process that will build trust and the frank and full sharing of information, in order that a fair, just, particularized, and lasting result can be reached. If he can, the negotiator should try to employ advanced empathy strate-gies of agreeing to the benefits of the problem-solving process.

Each should present his case in a manner that tries to fairly de-scribe how each sees the situation. To the extent that each can either concede weakness or admit to the strength of the other side's position, they can build trust. Also, to the extent that each bargainer can demon-strate that he is listening to the others, and open to changing his view of the case, if a fair problem-solving approach can be reached, the bargain-ers will be better able to reach a particularized result that maximizes the creative win/win solutions that are possible.

E. Democratic Theory and Multi-Party Dispute Resolution

Problems-solvers in a multi-party negotiation setting are more in-terested in setting up a process that places great faith in the principles of representative democracy. They argue that coalitions and enclaves of like-minded, fear-driven bargainers, are likely to engage in "group tough" talk and polarize the discussions by taking extreme positions. It is better to let the deliberative process take place, informed by the reasoned positions of all the diverse interests in the outcome, for a lasting and creative solution to be reached.

Once again, the adversarial position bargaining problem-solving distinction is also helpful in determining whether a mediator might help the parties design a fair process that will help facilitate the best result. When a mediator is skilled at position bargaining, and an expert evaluator, then the mediator can help position bargainers and start to assess the value of the case and risks in the end game. These mediators can also help the parties form coalitions in order to move an intransient bargainer to settlement. (Professor Francis McGovern, who mediates classes of asbestos cases, is the classic example of this kind of mediator. In the asbestos litigation, his success occurred in delivering classes of claimants to the defendants. He negotiated fixed numbers of claimants and average amounts of plaintiff's damages in exchange for certainty and finality for the defendants.)

The neutral problem-solving mediator brings other skills to the mediation. The neutral problem-solver will bring a process that builds trust. The parties may be asked to sign an agreement that they will engage in a full and complete exchange of information. The neutral problem-solver may suggest that other parties be brought into the negotiation, to insure that representative democracy really takes place. (Reaching an agreement between the state government and a polluter that does not take into account the interests of those who live down stream, in a different state, will not last very long.) The information exchange will include an exchange of the underlying goals and objectives of the parties. The neutral problem-solving mediator will then engage the parties in brainstorming alternative solutions, and help them get the information to predict consequences. The neutral problem-solving mediator will be interested in designing a monitoring system for whatever solution is selected, to insure that the solution is being implemented in the fair and reasonable way according to the parties.

Such a process of joint deliberation also avoids the problems that arise from the phenomenon of *group polarization*. Group polarization occurs when those who think similarly discuss their views of what happened only with each other, and become more convinced of their view, less tolerant of other views, and less empathetic to the perspectives of concerns of those who are not in their group. It is important for parties to realize the potential biasing affects of entering into alliances or side deals with other like-minded defendants or plaintiffs. The loss in trust of the other side, the polarizing biased and radical presentation of the case can lead to deadlock. That is why it may be better to engage in a negotiation with all the affected parties as to the democratic process that will be used to explore the facts and fairly attribute responsibility, rather than seek strategic combinations that may lead to deadlock and distrust.[21]

Problem 10.1

In the *Green v. Hall and Rose* negotiation, the plaintiff is a black couple seeking damages, an apology, and assurances that the discrimination they experienced, does not happen again. They had submitted an offer through Hall to Rose, for Rose's home. Hall, the broker, communicated the Greens offer, and assured the Green's it would be accepted. Rose received a second higher bid from another prospective buyer. The prospective buyer was white. Rose accepted the higher bid, without giving the Greens a chance to counter offer. In depositions of Hall and Rose, each blames the other for what happened, attributing racist motives to the other. If you represented Hall, would you now still seek to reach a coalition with Rose before you entered into negotiations with Green? In the alternative, what process might Green, Rose, and Hall agree to that would fairly lead to the resolution of the dispute? How might this negotiated process differ from traditional adjudication?

---

21 Cass R. Sunstein, *Deliberative Trouble: Why Some Groups Go to Extremes*, YALE L. J. 71 (2000).

Multi-Party Negotiations **Adversarial Approaches**	Multi-Party Negotiations **Problem-solving Approaches**
• Enter coalitions or jt defense agreements • Position, bargain, and block information exchanged • Test opposition through classic position bargaining • Use representative adjudications, focus group results to predict and persuade outcomes • Use bankruptcy to protect key assets, dismiss punitive damages, and limit future claimants • Suggest solutions that party controls (arbitration before sympathetic arbitrator)	• Identify, research salient features, history of dispute • Use principles of democratic theory to identify all stakeholders' representatives, and design a process that will likely produce a fair result • Select fair, distinguished mediator • Make early concession to demonstrate good faith • Look for win-win creative solutions • Enlist mediator in proposing solutions • Cooperative and participate in monitoring settlement solution(s)

CHAPTER 11
CULTURAL CONSIDERATIONS AND NEGOTIATIONS

In an increasingly global marketplace, it is vital that lawyer negotiators understand the role that cultural differences can play in conducting negotiations. There is a great deal of evidence that suspicion and hostility between parties from different cultures can inadvertently be fueled by remarks and actions that negotiators interpret as insulting and offensive and reflecting badly on their honor. The ability to implement your client's ends will often depend on the lawyer's ability to anticipate these differences and choose the right approach for the right setting.

In general, preparation regarding cultural considerations needs to include the examination of one's own cultural chauvinism. A party is chauvinistic if his or her view is egotistic and self-centered: the view that a toddler has of the world, that he is the center of attention, and that the world revolves around his happiness. On a related matter, the parties need to examine their ethnocentrism. By this, we mean the parties need to examine not only their ethnic perspectives, but also their religious, racial, or national characteristics, especially their subconscious beliefs about the importance of the individual and the particular values imbedded in each party ethnicity.

One of the most important values to examine is the tolerance of each party for the other's cultural differences. Inherent cultural differences are often viewed through the lens of each party and create a bias that each is being more practical and realistic about the way the world works. Each may appear to minimize differences but lack real understanding of how the particular cultural lens will distort each party's position to the other. Examination of yourself and your own stereotypes of the other party will help prepare you to be sensitive to cultural differences and their impact on your strategic decision making.

A. The Japanese Experience as a Paradigm

In recent decades when the Japanese economy was booming, American business, and U.S. Government, was particularly enamored with Japan business. In trade negotiations between the U.S. and Japan, to open Japanese markets to U.S. manufacturers, the experience of U.S. negotiators was cited as a reason to take cultural differences seriously in negotiating with foreigners. In a gross oversimplification of the negotiations between the parties, the negotiations went something like this: The head of the U.S. delegation led off and made persuasive statements in support of why the Japanese needed to give equal shelf space to U.S. products as they gave to Japanese products, how the U.S. did the same with Japanese goods, how free trade demanded fair goods placement, and how everyone was better off because the market would then be better able to make quality and price comparisons for the betterment of the customers in both countries.

All during the presentations the Japanese negotiators listened respectfully. They nodded, in apparent agreement. They even said Yes, with enthusiasm as the American negotiators made their points. The U.S. delegation went back to their rooms that night fully believing that they had convinced the Japanese of their positions. In the days and weeks that followed however, the U.S. determined that the Japanese delegation was not persuaded. They, in fact, learned that the Japanese delegation was not calling the shots; that there was an "undisclosed principal negotiator" who was behind the scenes and refusing to move. The U.S. delegation announced agreements, only to learn that there had been no agreement. Similar experiences were reported in negotiations between U.S. and Japanese businesses.

At first, the cultural differences were described in somewhat racist terms: that you could not trust the Japanese, that they were tricky, and inscrutable. But over time, a number of cultural differences explained the negotiation experience. Seen in the light of our position bargaining and problem-solving paradigms, they became quite understandable.

Commentators have written books explaining the different cultural values that underlie the Japanese business experience.[22] At the heart of the difference between negotiation styles and strategies is the concept of the Japanese "Wa." *Wa* is a deeply ingrained system of princi-

---

22 Yumi Adachi, Business Negotiations Between the Americans and the Japanese, Global Business Languages, (1997); Rober M. March, The Japanese Negotiator: Subtlety and Strategy Beyond Western Logic, Kodansha International (1990); Kazuo Nishiyama, Doing Business with Japan: Successful Strategies for Intercultural Communication, University of Hawaii Press, (2000); Alan Goldman, Doing Business with the Japanese: A Guide to Successful Communication, Management, and Diplomacy, State University of New York Press, (1994); Boye DeMente, Japanese Etiquette & Ethics in Business, Lincolnwood, (1994).

ples designed to promote interpersonal harmony, mutual trust, respect, responsibility, unselfish cooperation, and loyalty among groups. While it can be seen similarly to religion (that the cynic would say oppresses the masses for the betterment of the few, powerful, and extremely wealthy), the Japanese promote *Wa* as a means of establishing the trusting relationships necessary for creativity, personal growth, and responsible accountable action that drive Japanese productivity and quality of product.

If *Wa* is the goal of any business relationship, then the Japanese negotiating style is understandable:

❖ First meetings should not talk about business, and should be purely social to emphasize the start of a new relationship between the parties and the importance of getting to know each other and understand each other's values.

❖ Exchange of business cards is a ritual.

❖ Any decision that will be reached by the Japanese will be a product of a business consensus. The parties to this consensus will include people drawn from every level of the business, including line workers, middle managers, and the highest officers. Each of these groups needs to understand it and feel right about the decision.

❖ A U.S. business delegation should also include members from all levels of the U. S. business. If these are people who will be in relationship with the Japanese business, then the Japanese need to get to know them. (Part of the business card ritual, helps to make the Japanese delegation understand that there is representation and relationships at all levels of the business.)

❖ Longevity of a negotiator, or party representative, with a business is especially important. It shows the importance of loyalty and commitment to the business that is necessary for the enhancement of *Wa*.

❖ Japanese don't mean yes, when they say yes, or no when they say no. The Japanese are more interested in reaching understanding, and promoting a good feeling during presentations of ideas. They do not want the opposing negotiator to be interrupted, embarrassed, or become defensive. The Japanese give agreeable responses or, "aizuchi," to make the other side's communication go smoothly and avoid making the other side feel embarrassed. In fact, it is common for the Japanese negotiator to lead off with the answer Yes, even when they disagree, as the disagreement will come in what follows the yes, as a refinement, modification, or reversal of what the other side has to say. Saying No, is too confrontational, and hurts the relationship. For a Japanese negotiator it is far better to change the subject then to say no.

❖ Eye contact is disrespectful. It interrupts the speaker to be concerned about the listener and affects the speaker's train of thought.

❖ Silence is respect. It allows the speaker to think and gather words and ideas to promote better understanding.

❖ Negotiations take time, as the goal is Wa, even where no deal can be reached. "Ningen Kankei" (warm interpersonal relationship) requires time and trust, and is put off by aggressive position bargaining, by parties with a limited understanding of or longevity with the business.

These commentators then suggest that American negotiators adopt the following tactics, if they want to be successful:

❖ Start slow. Develop relationships and trust first, and then talk business.

❖ Take a team approach and include negotiators from all levels on your team.

❖ Recognize the persons with authority may not even be present at first and that any big business decision will likely be made by consensus and needs to be supported by reasons appealing to those in all levels of the business.

❖ American negotiators should develop a vague and general style up front. They should speak in terms of goals and broad objectives. (They should develop the language of problem-solving.)

B. The Chinese

Imagine doing business in the following environment. There is no "rule of law." If a person breaks a promise there are little real consequences to your broken promise. If you would go to court, the judge would not likely be law trained. The judge would be open to being directly influenced by the political party in control of national and local government. The contract law provides for freedom of contract, but makes an exception for the enforceability of the contract if "public policy" dictates otherwise. (On its face, not all that different from U.S. contract law, except that there is no developed system of case precedent that describes unconscionability, and when a contract might be unenforceable and there is no common practice whereby a U.S. judge will call the "party" to determine whether this is a "policy" against or in favor of the contract, as there is in the Chinese setting.) Your lawyer would not be allowed in court. You are entitled to a "friend," as is your opposition. Of course, a party might pick a friend to whom the judge is beholden for their job, or who runs the local government, or who knows how any judgment might negatively affect the community. Even if you got a judgment from the court, the finality of the judgment would be open to question. In addition, the enforcement of the judgment would be open, as the official tasked with enforcement is its own entity, with limited notions of private property. Levying on assets would also raise its own set of questions.

Imagine further that business practices provide little in the way of transparency, or a way for a bargainer to know the financial condition of the person with whom they are bargaining. There is little in the way of accounting records. Relationships with creditor and financiers (State Banks) are hard to document, and are very uncertain because the lending institutions themselves are hard to examine for their financial condition.

In these circumstances, if you want to do business your bargainer is left to bargain out of the shadow of the law, or in anything like the conditions that most businesses in the West are used to dealing. In these situations, one can see why the Japanese-like style of negotiation, based on the "Wa" would develop.

When you enter into a relationship without the automatic enforcement mechanisms of contract damages, and specific performance, you are left in a state of continued negotiation. Even if you have agreed on a dispute resolution forum and/or choice of law for enforcement that is more predictable (i.e., international arbitration in Hong Kong, where principles of English common law have developed a body of Hong Kong Chinese case law that can be used), you still have problems of enforcing those decisions on the mainland in China. Whatever you "agree" to up front is just a starting point if either side does not perform. Your only remedy is to "renegotiate" the terms of the relationship in light of whatever new conditions have arisen. This is what negotiators contend with in China.

Of course, the situation in China is evolving. China has a new constitution. It is developing a system of laws that can be known by its judges. It is developing a role for lawyers. It is "committed" to the development of the rule of law by the training of judges. Because its businesses want to do business in the west (for example Chinese furniture businesses want to sell furniture in California), it needs its own lawyers to understand Western law and Western style of negotiations. As these businesses do business with the West they develop models of contract that are affected by the Western understanding of efficient enforcement and rule of law. China has joined the WTO and seems to understand that International UCC and rule of law principles lower transaction costs, encourage investment, and globalization of market place takes place. Still, until the rule of law advances sufficiently in China, the problem gathering information, judging risk, and managing gains necessitates a "Japanese" style of negotiation. People seeking to do business in China must develop a relationship of trust. They must go slow and understand the underlying goals and aspirations of the business persons they are dealing with. They must learn who controls the business and who makes the decisions. They must develop either enough trust, or a set of processes to build trust, that the risks they entail are balanced by the gains they can expect.

As with the Japanese paradigm (and maybe Chinese experience helps us understand how the Japanese models of negotiation developed), the advice for U.S. negotiators is to be more problem-solving in their approach.

❖ Develop first the process of gathering information and communicating about and dealing with expected income and costs, rather than on pricing the deals.

❖ Prepare a clear understanding of your own goals.

❖ Seek a relationship that will help you get information about the opposing side's goals and objectives.

❖ Take the time to get to know the other side's business, and for them to get to know yours.

❖ Lengthen the time you expect to take to reach a deal.

Do not start with an extreme offer and expect that the other side will be used to position bargaining, and there will be no loss of credibility, if you move off your opening position.

❖ Make an early initial concession as a demonstration of your good faith.

❖ Seek to learn from each other how to best fulfill the shared goals of each side.

❖ Brainstorm alternative arrangements and their consequences.

❖ Initially, state positions tentatively and hypothetically, so that no face is lost either by the acceptance of the term and later inability to live up to it, or by the rejection of the term in its initial offering.

❖ Cooperate in reaching a consensus on what would work best. Involve decision makers at all levels in both your businesses.

❖ Look at joint paying arrangements for employees.

❖ Offer positions to prominent Chinese business persons on the board of your company, just as you might with a major U.S. business who was important to your business.

❖ Use national Chinese negotiators (trained in the U. S. in the ways of U.S. business) as the face of your business.

❖ Develop monitoring mechanisms with the Chinese business to get both sides' information about how well the deal is working. This will allow you the ability to adjust the terms of the deal before a dispute arises and the relationship of trust is affected by the dispute itself.

C. The Palestinians

Image you are a Palestinian. You grew up learning about the way that your parents and grandparents were treated when Israel was established. The version you were told is that when U.S. and Europe offered Israel a homeland that your parents were promised, when they were moved from their homes, that they would soon be able to return. Since then, through a number of wars with Egypt, Syria, Jordan, and Lebanon, various promises were made by the West for your family to return to their homeland. None of these promises have been kept. You understand that the reason they have not been kept is said to be issues of security and the right of Israel to exist. You believe the right of Israel to exist depends first on the return of your family to the land unlawfully taken from them. You do business in this cultural environment. How would it affect your strategy and tactics of negotiation?

On the one hand, you might take your lesson from how you were treated, especially when dealing with the west. You make promises when it is convenient in order to get what you want. You believe it is unnecessary to fulfill your promises if it is inconvenient for you do so. You are not lying. You believe in the principles of efficient breach.

Your level of distrust is great. You are only willing to enter into deals with people you trust. Trust is much more than taking positions and making promises. Trust has to born out by action and sacrifice. But once that trust is earned, the loyalty will be worth the time spent in building the trust.

To the westerner, with western expectations, the Palestinian bargainer is more adversarial and position bargaining in strategy then they are. The culture helps explains where the stereotype might come from: that Palestinians lie, that they renege on their promises, that they are angry and emotional bargainers, taking exceptions to the mildest threats, and are quick to escalate the bargaining and resort to deadlock and violence if need be. Issues of saving face are of utmost importance.

Some argue that the only way to deal with position bargainers is by positioning bargaining, and strict agreement enforcement. Others believe that problem-solving strategies offer more hope, especially where the time is taken to build trust by building principles and processes for dealing with future disputes. (See intractable disputes. Cf. Ireland and Dayton Peace accords)

D. The Caution of Black South Africans

In the mid-1990s after apartheid ended in South Africa the U.S. State Department and USAID developed a program for the development of business and government leaders among black South Africans. The program was designed to bring groups of 40–50 black South Africans to the U.S. for special training. They started at the Wharton School, for instruction in finance, then they went to New York and Wall Street, and then to Washington, D.C., for a course in negotiation training.

One of us had the privilege of teaching a course in negotiation and on a number of occasions during the teaching of the course, some version of the following experience was relayed that raises a significant caution for problem-solving negotiators:

> I'm so happy to be taking this course. I'm in desperate need of learning how to negotiate like you in the West. You see my family has long run a business in South Africa. After apartheid ended, we were approached by a western business. They told us they were very interested in seeing us succeed. They want black South African business to lead Africa into prosperity. They asked us how they could help. They wanted to know all about our business: our suppliers, our customers, our marketing approaches, our sources of finance, our manufacturing process, everything about our business. After we spent an enormous time with them, they left. We did not hear from them. After about a year we came across them again. It turns out that they had taken the information we gave them and used it to set up a competing business here in South Africa. Sure, they may have hired a black South African, to be the face of the business, but in reality, they were never negotiating with us in good faith at all. We want to learn those techniques, so that we can protect ourselves and use them on others.

The warning for all bargainers is clear. There are risks to "problem-solving" strategies if the other side is not negotiating in good faith. Trust is not something that is developed risk free. And a lie dressed up like trust, looks like trust. So to, a position bargainer dressed up like a problem-solver, looks and acts like a problem-solver. In the words of the immortal George Burns, "Once you learn how to fake sincerity, everything else comes easy."

So we recommend, in the end, a functional approach to bargaining, whether in the international arena, public or private, or in litigation or national or local business setting. Just as cultural differences form the lens through which each bargainer sees the bargaining process, so does the personality of the individual bargainer and the strategy they have adopted, form the lens by which they act and respond to the bargaining process.

Both strategies need to be used to control the flow of information, what you give and what you get. Position bargaining does not depend on trust and derives information from the moves that people make. Deadlines and threats, deadlocks and walk outs, strikes and even violence reveal information about the other side's strengths, weaknesses, goals, and objectives.

Problem-solvers can cut through the inefficiencies of bargaining in the context of distrust, where the rule of law provides an after-the-fact deterrence on the behavior of the parties. It allows the parties the potential to grow to *Wa,* and experience the harmony and joy of long-term creative relationships built on trust. At risk, however, is a bet on your judgment of human nature. Does the other side really care about your growth and happiness? What if it is better for them financially or otherwise to enter into a different relationship with someone else? Can you ever really trust them to not cause you harm whenever a combination of a better offer and "getting away with it" arises? For these reasons the problem-solver needs to be able to access the probabilities and risks, and determine what position needs to be their bottom line. Just as an abused spouse needs to be able to walk out as a matter of personal integrity, so too, the problem-solver needs to understand position bargaining to enforce and maintain his or her integrity.

CHAPTER 12
ETHICAL CONSIDERATIONS

Usually, negotiators prefer not to disclose everything at a negotiation's outset and want to influence the direction the negotiation goes to some extent. Even cooperative problem-solvers do not initially disclose everything and are interested in steering the negotiation, or at least the process the negotiation follows, in a particular direction. Competitive adversarial negotiators might be more blunt. They seek to mislead the other side, at least as to their real bottom line, and they seek to manipulate the other side to achieve their goals. Given this setting, negotiation raises a number of ethical issues that should not be a surprise. Chief among the ethical issues in negotiation is how truthful you must be. In this chapter, we will discuss this issue and raise additional ethical considerations of which you should be aware.

A. Truthfulness

The most troubling ethical issue in negotiation is lying. A fundamental assumption of negotiation is that the participants resist revealing at least some information to the other side. To be sure, during information bargaining, adversarials emphasize seeking and hiding information whereas problem-solvers emphasize seeking and revealing information. In Chapter 6, we discussed the tactics associated with "blocking" the disclosure of information. At what point does this attempt to avoid disclosure become unethical? Unfortunately, no clear answer exists.

Problem 12.1

The lawyers for Green have been authorized to settle the lawsuit with Hall and Rose for $10,000 plus a public apology. During face-to-face negotiations, may the lawyers for Green ethically state: "My client has authorized to settle for nothing less than $250,000. That's our bottom line. Accept it or we will see you in court."?

Problem 12.1 raises the basic question of whether negotiation statements concerning what your client will find acceptable are subject to a truthfulness standard. The American Bar Association Model Rules of Professional Conduct provide only general statements concerning the obligation to be truthful. Model Rule 4.1 provides:

In the course of representing a client a lawyer shall not:

(a) Knowingly make a false statement of fact or law to a third person; or

(b) Knowingly fail to disclose a fact to a third person when:

(1) In the circumstances failure to make disclosure is equivalent to making a material misrepresentation;

(2) Disclosure is necessary to prevent assisting a criminal or fraudulent act, as required by Rule 1.2(d); or

(3) Disclosure is necessary to comply with the law.

Model Rule 4.1(b) provides little more guidance than the admonition that lawyers shall not fail to disclose when such failure is in violation of legal requirements to disclose. Subparagraph (a), however, with its broad prohibition against making a false statement has significantly more potential for suggesting ethical restrictions. What the drafters actually contemplated by the phrase "knowingly make a false statement" is, however, not at all clear. A comment to Rule 4.1 in fact states, "Under generally accepted conventions in negotiation, certain types of statements ordinarily are not taken as statements of material fact. Estimates of price or value placed on the subject of a transaction and a party's intentions as to an acceptable settlement of a claim are in this category...."

Under the commentary to the Model Rules, it appears clear that counsel's statements in Problem 12.1 are ethically permissible. However, relying on conventions—as the community does—to determine what is permissible is problematic at best. A number of problems are readily apparent. What community of lawyers should we look at to determine the conventions? Do the conventions in one geographical area apply across the country, much less the state or the city? Even within a geographical area, do lawyers in different types of practices have different conventions? Are the conventions different for criminal defense attorneys, for example, than for securities lawyers?

In light of the ambiguity of the standard, a couple of points must be made. First, you should not assume that your interpretation of existing conventions is the same as opposing counsel's. A little skepticism is not a bad thing. Certain conduct crosses the line and constitutes unethical or even illegal behavior. However, you should recognize that negotiation is among the most private activities a lawyer does and you cannot count on the bar ethics committee to be looking over your opponent's shoulder.

Second, some guidance is nonetheless available. The Model Rule's commentary that "[e]stimates of price or value placed on the subject of a transaction and a party's intentions as to an acceptable settlement of a claim are in this category...." suggests that a useful distinction can be made between statements concerning historical facts on the one hand and interpretations, inferences, or intentions. A statement that a client has received twenty stitches as a result of the accident when he only received ten concerns a historic, objectively verifiable fact, and is a lie. A statement that the client will not accept less than $250,000 in satisfaction of his claim, when after counseling the client has indicated he would accept as little as $10,000 plus a public apology, is puffing and would generally be considered permissible.

B. Other Ethical Considerations

A number of other professional responsibility issues, none unique to negotiation, should be kept in mind.

Model Rules of Professional Conduct Rule 1.1 provides that "[a] lawyer shall provide competent representation to a client. Competent representation requires the legal knowledge, skill, thoroughness, and preparation reasonably necessary for the representation." The obligation to provide competent representation obviously is not unique to negotiation. You should remember, however, that competence is more than facility with doctrinal analysis. Competence in the context of a negotiation requires negotiation skill, just as competence in the context of a trial lawyer requires courtroom skill.

Problem 12.2

Assume in Problem 12.1 plaintiff's counsel responds by saying, "That offer is insulting. I'm not even going to dignify it by taking it back to my client." Is there an ethical problem?

To the extent that the lawyer in Problem 12.2 does not take the settlement offer back to Popcheck, there appears to be an ethical problem. Model Rules of Professional Conduct Rule 1.2(a) provides that "[a] lawyer shall abide by a client's decision whether to accept an offer of settlement of a matter. In a criminal case, the lawyer shall abide by the client's decision, after consultation with the lawyer, as to a plea to be entered, whether to waive jury trial and whether the client will testify." The Model Rules clearly make the decision on whether to accept a legitimate settlement offer the client's—not the lawyer's. Indeed, the Model Rules make it clear that the lawyer has an affirmative obligation to ensure that the client has sufficient information upon which to base this decision: "a lawyer negotiating on behalf of a client should provide the client with facts relevant to the matter, inform the client of communications from another party and take other reasonable steps that permit the client to make a decision regarding a serious offer from another party." Model Rules of Professional Conduct Rule 1.4.

Problem 12.3

Assume that in Problem 12.2 defense counsel is convinced that plaintiff's counsel has not communicated the $250,000 offer to Popcheck. May defense counsel contact her directly with the offer?

As just discussed, Model Rules 1.2 and 1.4 require a client's decision concerning a serious settlement offer. Problem 12.3, however, raises the question of what can be done by opposing counsel if she believes the offer has not been communicated to the other party. On occasion, a lawyer will feel frustrated, thinking that a legitimate offer they have put on the table has not been taken back to the client. The solution is, however, not to bypass opposing counsel and communicate directly to the opposing party. Model Rules of Professional Conduct Rule 4.2 states: "In representing a client, a lawyer shall not communicate about the subject of the representation with a party the lawyer knows to be represented by another lawyer in the matter, unless the lawyer has the consent of the other lawyer or is authorized by law to do so."

The options available to you to get the offer to an opposing party are therefore limited. Asking your client to contact the other client is not an option in a litigation setting, because you cannot circumvent an ethical proscription through the actions of a third person. If suit has been filed and the jurisdiction has a provision similar to Federal Rule of Civil Procedure 68's offer of judgment, invoking the rule may provide some help in this situation. Rule 68 provides in part, "[a]t any time more than 10 days before the trial begins, a party defending against a claim may serve upon the adverse party an offer to allow judgment...against the defending party...for the money...specified in the offer." If the offer is not accepted, and the offeree ultimately recovers less than the offer, the offeree must pay all costs subsequent to the offer. The effect of the provision for our purposes is that it increases the likelihood opposing counsel will at least communicate an offer made subject to Rule 68.

General provisions concerning confidentiality and conflict of interest, of course, affect the lawyer in negotiation. In particular, Model Rules of Professional Conduct Rule 1.8(g) provides that "[a] lawyer who represents two or more clients shall not participate in making an aggregate settlement of the claims of or against the clients...unless each client consents after consultation, including disclosure of the existence and nature of all the claims...involved and the participation of each person in the settlement." This Rule makes clear what should probably already be clear from general provisions governing conflicts of interest and the client's right to accept or reject settlement offers.

A final consideration concerns Model Rules of Professional Conduct Rule 4.4, which prohibits conduct intended to humiliate and harass. Competitive negotiators, in particular, must be aware of the line between aggressive advocacy and harassment. Crossing that line may not only affect your effectiveness, but be unethical.

Problem 12.4

Assume that negotiations in *Green v. Hall and Rose* have been conducted over a number of weeks. You are approaching trial. You represent Hall. Remember that Hall has had her deposition taken and has denied having a racial motive for not taking the Green's offer. In recent conversations with Hall, she refuses to pay more and expresses that part of her reasoning was and is racist. May Hall's attorney settle the case without revealing that Hall lied during her deposition?

Traditionally, lawyers have taken the position that the risk of a deposition was that no automatic duty arose to supplement if facts testified to in a deposition changed after the deposition and before trial. If a witness admitted giving false testimony, the remedy was to settle the case without revealing the fact of the false testimony.

Recent changes to the Model Rule 3.3 have called this practice into question. Model Rule 3.3 speaks to Candor toward the Tribunal. It provides:

(a) A Lawyer shall not knowingly:

> **(1)** make a false statement of fact or law to a tribunal or fail to correct a false statement of material fact or law previously made to the tribunal

> **(2)**...

> **(3)** offer evidence that the lawyer knows to be false. If a lawyer, the lawyer's client, or a witness called by the lawyer, has offered material evidence and the lawyer comes to know of its falsity, the lawyer shall take reasonable remedial measures, including, if necessary, disclosure to the tribunal.

While early Model Rules were unclear whether a statement in a deposition was a statement to a tribunal, the comments recently enacted make it clear that a deposition is a statement to a tribunal.

Comment 1 to 3.3 provides:

> [1] This Rule governs the conduct of a lawyer who is representing a client in the proceedings of a tribunal. See Rule 1.0(m) for the definition of "tribunal." It also applies when the lawyer is representing a client in an ancillary proceeding conducted pursuant to the tribunal's adjudicative authority, such as a deposition. Thus, for example, paragraph (a)(3) requires a lawyer to take reasonable remedial measures if the lawyer comes to know that a client who is testifying in a deposition has offered evidence that is false.

As a result, the Model Rule 3.4 specifies the action that the lawyer is supposed to take if he learns that false testimony has been given in a deposition. The lawyer is to remonstrate with the client, and take reasonable remedial measures. If the client does not agree to reveal the fraud to the other side, the lawyer must move to withdraw. The implication is that the lawyer cannot settle the case without withdrawal or revealing to the other side the false statement at the deposition.

C. Conclusion

As much if not more than anything else a lawyer does, negotiation is usually a very private activity. The client is counseled in private and the lawyers sit down face-to-face in private. The result may be public, but the process is quite closed. As such, inappropriate behavior will not likely be subject to outside review. Just imagine, for example, the difficulty of filing a complaint with a state bar ethics group and then proving that opposing counsel has lied to you during the negotiation. Negotiation, like so much else a lawyer does, therefore, relies heavily on the individual ethics of the participants involved. You should keep in mind that your ethical conduct with a client or an opponent in a negotiation will pay dividends to both your professional reputation and your future dealings with these people.

Adversarial Approaches to Ethical Dilemmas	Problem-Solving Approaches to Ethical Dilemmas
• Counsel client into not giving negotiator "knowledge" of bad fact • On questions of intent to settle, represent the parties intent in whatever way best serves the negotiator's position-bargaining strategy • On questions of value, represent value in whatever way best serves the negotiator's position-bargaining strategy • Using agenda control and multiple blocking strategies • Rule questions out of bounds • Refer to what is on the record or "before the court" in answer to questions concerning vulnerabilities	• Investigate facts to discover vulnerabilities before formal discovery starts • Engage in client counseling to get permission to reveal vulnerabilities as a strategy of showing good faith and reasonableness • Trade information on vulnerabilities • Brainstorm with clients re creative solutions to resolve dispute and produce fair results • Think strategically for how to protect what is vital and essential and deal fairly with opponent's legitimate needs

APPENDIX
PREPARATION AND PLANNING WORKSHEET

Your Goals

— What do you wish to accomplish?

— What are you willing to accept?

Their Goals

— What do you believe the other party seeks to accomplish?

— What do you believe the other party would be willing to accept?

Adversarial or problem-solving or a combination?

— What advantages do each strategy have in this particular negotiation?

— If you are going to approach the negotiation from an adversarial perspective, what is your bottom line at this point?

— What will you use as a starting position?

— What facts do you have that might indicate

the likely starting position of the other side?

the likely bottom line of the other side?

— Can you plot the potential bargaining ranges on each side?

— What information do you have available that would suggest the other side's probable strategy (adversarial, problem-solving or some mix)?

— What facts do you have that might indicate

the underlying needs, interests, and desires of the other side?

the probable proposals the other side might make?

— Are you aware of any social or psychological facts that might impact this negotiation?

— If you are willing to shift strategy during the negotiation, what factors will motivate you to switch? How will you make the switch?

For example, if you wish to move from adversarial to problem-solving, what actions can you plan to take to increase trust or decrease the risk associated with problem-solving?

— What information can you seek from sources other than a face-to-face meeting with the other person?

— Is this negotiation best accomplished face-to-face, by telephone, by letter, or some combination? Why?

— If the negotiation is face-to-face, where will it take place? Why?

— If you control the setting of the negotiation, how will you arrange the location?

— How long will the negotiation take? Why?

— In this particular phase of the negotiation do you seek to accomplish all of your goals, or will this have a more limited purpose? For example, is this meeting only to obtain information or merely to begin developing a rapport?

— Are there any conventions or controlling principles you need to consider in this negotiation?

— How will you establish the agenda?

    — How will you establish what to negotiate?

    — How will you establish the manner in which you negotiate?

— What type of ice breaking will you use, if any? Why?

— What information do you need to get from the other person? Why?

    — How will you get this information?

    — What questions will you ask to get information from the other person?

    — In what order will you ask the questions?

    — What information is the other side likely to seek from you?

    — What information is the other side likely to try and avoid giving you?

    — What will you do if the other person asks you for information you do not want to reveal?

    — What will you do if the person refuses to give you a piece of information either by blocking or outright refusal?

    — What will you do if the person tells you what you know to be a lie?

    — What information do you need to give the other side and how will you give it?

— What type of persuasive statements will you make?

— Can you identify objective criteria that supports the likely positions you will take or proposed solutions you will make?

— What are the possible criteria to be used by the other side?

— How will you respond to them?

— What are the details of your persuasive elements?

— Can you make your persuasive statements multidimensional? balanced? emphatic?

— Are there any points that must be subtle?

— Do you anticipate any threats?

— How will you respond to threats?

— What type of concessions are you willing to consider?

— What will you need to convince you a concession is appropriate?

— How will you respond if any of the following tactics is used against you?

Anger

Aggression

Boulwareism

Uneven number of negotiators

False demands

Attempts to get you to make the first offer

Attempts to get you to negotiate against yourself

Time pressure

— Will you use any of these tactics? Why?

— If it appears you are going to deadlock, what might you do?

— When will you likely end this negotiation?

— How will you likely end this negotiation?

— Is one of your goals to monitor how the settlement is working?

> If so, how will this be done?
>
> Who will report to whom about what?
>
> What happens if they don't report?
>
> What happens if a dispute arises?

— Do the parties want to decide now on how future disputes will be resolved?

POST NEGOTIATION WORKSHEET

Did you accomplish your goals? Why? Why not?

Were you able to set the tone that you desired for the negotiation? Why or why not?

Did you control the agenda? Why or why not?

Did you find as much information as you wanted? Why or why not?

Did you reveal too much information? Why or why not?

Did you fail to reveal information you should have? Why or why not?

If you did not agree, was it appropriate given the context of this particular negotiation? Why or why not?

If you have deadlocked, what might you be able to do to break that deadlock? Why or why not?

If you have deadlocked, might any of the issues in dispute profit from mediation? Would you want a neutral facilitative mediator or an evaluative mediator?

If you agreed, is the result fair, just, and equitable from everyone's perspective? Why or why not?

For each stage of the negotiation process that you conducted, what did you learn from this negotiation:

Preparation and Planning

Ice Breaking

Agenda Control

Information Bargaining

Offers/Demands/Proposals

Persuasion

Concessions/Reformulations

Crisis

Closing

Memorialization

What is the one thing you will do differently in the next negotiation?
Why?

SELECTED BIBLIOGRAPHY

The following list of articles and books is not meant to be an exhaustive bibliography. Also, the list is not meant to imply we agree with what the material has to say about negotiation. In fact, we do not agree with everything that is said in these books and articles, but they provide additional detail, and sometimes a different perspective which can further your understanding of the negotiation process.

Articles

Robert S. Adler & Elliot M. Silverstein, *When David Meets Goliath: Dealing With Power Differentials in Negotiations*, 5 HARV. NEGOT. L. REV. 1 (2000).

Ian Ayres & Barry J. Nalebuff, *Common Knowledge as a Barrier to Negotiation*, 44 UCLA L. REV. 1631 (1997).

John Barkai, *Teaching Negotiation and ADR: The Savvy Samurai Meets the Devil*, 75 NEB. L. REV. 704 (1996).

Gary S. Berman, *Facilitated Negotiation: An Effective ADR Technique*, 50 DISP. RESOL. J. 18 (1995).

Gary S. Berman, *Facilitating Construction Negotiations*, 50 DISP. RESOL. J. 23 (1995).

Richard Birke and Craig R. Fox, *Psychological Principles in Negotiating Civil Settlements*, 4 HARV. NEGOT. L. REV. 1 (1999).

Wayne D. Brazil, *Protecting the Confidentiality of Settlement Negotiations*, 39 HASTINGS L. J. 955 (1988).

Marshall J. Breger, *Should an Attorney be Required to Advise a Client of ADR Options?*, 13 GEO. J. LEGAL ETHICS 427 (2000).

Jennifer Gerarda Brown, *The Role of Hope in Negotiation*, 44 UCLA L. REV. 1661 (1997).

Cash and Janda, *The Eye of the Beholder*, PSYCHOL. TODAY 46, Dec. 1984.

Jonathan R. Cohen, *Reasoning Along Different Lines: Some Varied Roles of Rationality in Negotiation and Conflict Resolution*, 3 HARV. NEGOT. L. REV. 111 (1998).

Robert J. Condlin, *Bargaining in the Dark: The Normative Incoherence of Lawyer Dispute Bargaining Role*, 51 MD. L. REV. 1 (1992).

Robert J. Condlin, *"Cases on Both Sides": Patterns of Argument in Legal Dispute-Negotiation*, 44 MD. L. REV. 65 (1985).

John W. Cooley, *The Geometries of Situation and Emotions and the Calculus of Change in Negotiation and Mediation*, 29 VAL. U. L. REV. 1 (1994).

Charles B. Craver, *Negotiation Ethics: How to be Deceptive Without Being Dishonest/How to be Assertive Without Being Offensive*, 38 S. TEX. L. REV. 713 (1997).

Charles B. Craver, *Effective Legal Negotiation and Settlement*, CB55 ALI-ABA 1 (1996).

Joseph L. Daly, *International Commercial Negotiation and Arbitration*, 22 HAMLINE J. PUB. L. & POL'Y 217 (2001).

Andrew F. Daugherty & Jennifer F. Reinganum, *Settlement Negotiations with Two sided Asymmetric Information: Model Duality, Information Distribution, and Efficiency*, 14 INT'L REV. L. & ECON. 283 (1994).

Luis Miguel Diaz, *Notes on Negotiation and Unlearning Legal Thinking*, 688 PLI/LIT 505 (2003).

W. Donohue, *An Empirical Framework For Examining Negotiation Processes and Outcomes, Communication Monographs,* Vol. 45, August (1978).

Lynn A. Epstein, *Cyber E-mail Negotiation vs. Traditional Negotiation: Will Cyber Technology Supplant Traditional Means of Settling Litigation*, 36 TULSA L. J. 839 (2001).

Mary Jo Eyster, *Clinical Teaching, Ethical Negotiation, and Moral Judgment*, 75 NEB. L. REV. 752 (1996).

Amy Farmer & Paul Pecorino, *Pretrial Negotiations with Asymmetric Information on Risk Preferences*, 14 INT'L REV. L. & ECON. 273 (1994).

A. Forough et al., *An Empirical Study of an Interactive, Session-orientated Computerized Negotiation Support System, Group Decision and Negotiation*, 4 (1995).

Lawrence J. Fox, *Those Who Worry About the Ethics of Negotiation Should Never be Viewed as Just Another Set of Service Providers*, 52 MERCER L. REV. 977 (2001).

Clark Freshman et al, *The Lawyer-Negotiator as Mood Scientist: What We Know and Don't Know About How Mood Relates to Successful Negotiation*, 2002 J. DISP. RESOL. 1 (2002).

Donald G. Gifford, *The Synthesis of Legal Counseling and Negotiation Models: Preserving Client centered Advocacy in the Negotiation Context*, 34 UCLA L. REV. 811 (1987).

Portor Goltz, *Settling the Score: Good Negotiation Skills Pave the Way for Better Settlements*, 82-AUG A.B.A. J. 90 (1996).

Samuel R. Gross & Kent D. Syverud, *Getting to No: A Study of Settlement Negotiations and the Selection of Cases for Trial*, 90 MICH. L. REV. 319 (1991).

Thomas F. Guernsey, *Truthfulness in Negotiation*, 17 U. RICH. L. REV. 99 (1982).

Milton Heumann & Jonathan M. Hyman, *Negotiation Methods and Litigation Settlement Methods in New Jersey: "You Can't Always Get What You Want"*, 12 OHIO ST. J. ON DISP. RESOL. 253 (1997).

Michael R. Hogan, *Judicial Settlement Conferences: Empowering the Parties to Decide Through Negotiation*, 27 WILLAMETTE L. REV. 429 (1991).

James R. Holbrook & Laura M. Gray, *Court-annexed Alternative Dispute Resolution*, 21 J. CONTEMP. L. 1 (1995).

Shi-Ling Hsu, *A Game-Theoretic Approach to Regulatory Negotiation and a Framework for Empirical Analysis*, 26 HARV. ENVTL. L. REV. 33 (2002).

Jonathan M. Hyman, *Trial Advocacy and Methods of Negotiation: Can Good Trial Advocates Be Wise Negotiators?*, 34 UCLA L. REV. 863 (1987).

Peter R. Jarvis & Bradley F. Tellam, *A Negotiation Ethics Primer for Lawyers*, 31 GONZ. L. REV. 549 (1995-96).

Peter A. Joy & Kevin C. McMunigal, *Disclosing Exculpatory Material in Plea Negotiations*, 16-FALL CRIM. JUST. 41 (2001).

Russell Korobkin, *A Positive Theory of Legal Negotiation*, 88 GEO. L.J. 1789 (2000).

Bailey H. Kuklin, *The Asymmetrical Conditions of Legal Responsibility in the Marketplace*, 44 U. MIAMI L. REV. 893 (1990).

The Law Lists: The Art of Negotiating, 81-JUN A.B.A. J. 90 (1995).

Alain Lempereur, *Negotiation and Mediation in France: The Challenge of Skill-based Learning and Interdisciplinary Research in Legal Education*, 3 HARV. NEGOT. L. REV. 151 (1998).

Lisa G. Lerman, *Lying to Clients*, 138 U. PA. L. REV. 659 (1990).

Patrick Emery Longan, *Symposium, Ethics in Settlement Negotiations: Foreword*, 52 MERCER L. REV. 807 (2001).

Gary T. Lowenthal, *A General Theory of Negotiation Process, Strategy and Behavior*, 31 U. KAN. L. REV. 69 (1982).

Kate Marquess, *Point, Click–Settle Quick: Online Negotiations Hailed for Efficiency, but Some Prefer Face to Face*, 86-APR ABA J. 82 (2000).

Craig A. McEwen & Roselle L. Wissler, *Finding Out if it is True: Comparing Mediation and Negotiation Through Research*, 2002 J. DISP. RESOL. 131 (2002).

Kevin C. McMunigal, *Disclosure and Accuracy in the Guilty Plea Process*, 40 HASTINGS L.J. 957 (1989).

Carrie Menkel Meadow, *Toward Another View of Legal Negotiation: The Structure of Problem solving*, 31 UCLA L. REV. 754 (1984).

Robert H. Mnookin, *Strategic Barriers to Dispute Resolution: A Comparison of Bilateral and Multilateral Negotiations*, 8 HARV. NEGOT. L. REV. 1 (2003).

Eleanor Holmes Norton, *Bargaining and the Ethic of Process*, 64 N.Y.U. L. REV. 493 (1989).

Curtis Nyquist, *A Spectrum Theory of Negotiability*, 78 MARQ. L. REV. 897 (1995).

K. O'Connor, *Motives and Cognitions in Negotiation: A Theoretical Integration and an Empirical Test*, THE INTERNATIONAL JOURNAL OF CONFLICT MANAGEMENT (1997).

K. O'Connor & A. Adams, *What Novices Think About Negotiation: A Content Analysis of Scripts*, NEGOTIATION JOURNAL, April (1999).

David Brainerd Parrish, COMMENT, *The Dilemma: Simultaneous Negotiation of Attorneys' Fees and Settlement in Class Actions*, 36 HOUS. L. REV. 531 (1999).

Rex R. Perschbacher, *Regulating Lawyers' Negotiations*, 27 ARIZ. L. REV. 75 (1985).

Don Peters, *Mapping, Modeling, and Critiquing: Facilitating Learning Negotiation, Mediation, Interviewing, and Counseling*, 48 FLA. ST. L. REV. 875 (1996).

Don Peters, *Forever Jung: Psychological Type Theory, the Myers Briggs Type Indicator and Learning Negotiation*, 42 DRAKE L. REV. 1 (1993).

Geoffrey M. Peters, *The Use of Lies in Negotiation*, 48 OHIO ST. L.J. 1 (1987).

Lynne H. Rambo, *Impeaching Lying Parties With Their Statements During Negotiation: Demysticizing the Public Policy Rationale Behind Evidence Rule 408 and the Mediation-privilege Statutes*, 75 WASH. L. REV. 1037 (2000).

N. Reiches & H. Harral, *Argument in Negotiation: A Theoretical and Empirical Approach*, Speech Monographs, Vol. 41 (March 1974).

Alvin B. Rubin, *A Causerie on Lawyers' Ethics in Negotiation*, 35 LA. L. REV. 577 (1975).

Ernest P. Sachs, 25-JUN Vt. B.J. & L. Dig. 46 (1999) (reviewing GREGG HERMANN, *The Joy Of Settlement: The Family Lawyer's Guide To Effective Negotiations And Settlement Strategies*, (1997)).

Andrea Kupfer Schneider, *Shattering Negotiation Myths: Empirical Evidence on the Effectiveness of Negotiation Style*, 7 HARV. NEGOT. L. REV. 143 (2002).

Roy Stuckey, *Understanding Casablanca: A Values-based Approach to Legal Negotiations*, 5 CLINICAL L. REV. 211 (1998).

L. Thompson, *Negotiation Behavior and Outcomes: Empirical Evidence and Theoretical Issues,* PSYCHOLOGICAL BULLETIN (1990), Vol 108, No 3, pg 515

S. Weiss-Wik, *Enhancing Negotiator's Successfulness - Self-help Books and Related Empirical Research*, JOURNAL OF CONFLICT RESOLUTION, Vol 27 No. 4 (Dec, 1983).

Gerald Wetlaufer, *The Ethics of Lying in Negotiations*, 75 IOWA L. REV. 1219 (1990).

Williams W. Wilkins, Jr., *Plea Negotiations, Acceptance of Responsibility, Role of the Offender, and Departures: Policy Decisions in the Promulgation of Federal Sentencing Guidelines*, 23 WAKE FOREST L. REV. 181 (1988).

Zakeria Mohammed Yacoob, Salient Features of the Negotiating Process, 52 SMU L. REV. 1579 (1999).

Douglas H. Yarn, *Lawyer Ethics in ADR and the Recommendations of Ethics 2000 to Revise the Model Rules of Professional Conduct: Considerations for Adoption and State Application*, 54 ARK. L. REV. 207 (2001).

Marguerite Zoghby, *The Prohibition of Communication with Adverse Parties in Civil Negotiations: Protecting Clients or Preventing Solutions?*, 14 GEO. J. LEGAL ETHICS 1165 (2001).

Selected Books

Harold I. Abramson, *Mediation Representation: Advocacy in a Problem-Solving Process* (NITA, 2004).

Jean Albert, *Negotiation Skills: A Handbook* (1986).

Karl Albrecht & Steve Albrecht, *Added Value Negotiating: The Breakthrough Method for Building Balanced Deals* (1993).

Tom Anastasi, *Personality Negotiating: Conflict Without Casualty* (1993).

Kare Anderson, *Getting What You Want: How to Reach Agreement and Resolve Conflict Every Time* (1993).

Joseph Auer & Charles Edison Harris, *Computer Contract Negotiations* (1981).

Kenneth J. Arrow Et Al., *Barriers to Conflict Resolution* (1995).

Association Of Labor Relations Agencies, *Labor-management Relations in the Public Sector: Redefining Collective Bargaining* (John L. Bonner ed., 1999).

Eileen F. Babbitt, *Jimmy Carter: The Power of Moral Persuasion in International Mediation, in When Talk Works: Profiles Of Mediators* (Deborah M. Kolb ed., 1994).

Samuel B. Bacharach & Edward J. Lawler, *Bargaining: Power, Tactics, and Outcomes* (1981).

Ginny Pearson Barnes, *Successful Negotiating: Letting the Other Person Have Your Way* (1998).

Ginny Pearson Barnes, *8 Steps for Highly Effective Negotiation: Letting the Other Person Have Your Way* (1995).

✓ Robert M. Bastress & Joseph D. Harbaugh, *Interviewing, Counseling, and Negotiating* (1990).

Max H. Bazerman & Margaret A. Neale, *Negotiating Rationally* (1992).

Bureau of National Affairs (Washington, D.C.), *What's New in Collective Bargaining Negotiations & Contracts: Patterns in Union Contracts* (1989).

Bureau of National Affairs (Washington, D.C.), *Collective Bargaining Negotiations and Contracts* (1979).

Neal W. Beckmann, *Negotiations: Principles and Techniques* (1977).

Gary Bellow & Bea Moulton, *The Lawyering Process: Negotiation* (1981).

Alfred Benjamin, *The Helping Interview* (1974).

Jacob Bercovitch, *Social Conflicts and Third Parties: Strategies of Conflict Resolution* (1984).

Eric Berne, *Games People Play: The Psychology of Human Relationships* (1964).

Sissela Bok, *Lying: Moral Choice in Public and Private Life* (1978).

Steven J. Brams & Alan D. Taylor, *The Win-Win Solution: Guaranteeing Fair Shares to Everybody* (1999).

Wayne D. Brazil, *Effective Approaches to Settlement: A Handbook for Lawyers and Judges* (1988).

Ed Brodow, *Negotiate with Confidence* (1996).

Earl Brooks & George S. Odiorne, *Managing by Negotiations* (1984).

Jimmy Carter, *Negotiation: An Alternative to Hostility* (1984).

Jimmy Carter, *Talking Peace: A Vision for the Next Generation* (1993).

Pierre Casse, *The One-hour Negotiator* (1992).

Ralph Charell, *How to Get the Upper Hand* (1978).

David Churchman, *Negotiation: Process, Tactics, Theory* (2d Ed. 1995).

David Churchman, *Negotiation Tactics* (1993).

Herb Cohen, *Negotiate This!: By Caring, But Not T-h-a-t Much* (2003).

Herb Cohen, *You Can Negotiate Anything* (1980).

Laurie S. Coltri, *Conflict Diagnosis and Alternative Dispute Resolution and Mediation* (2004).

Charles Craver, *The Intelligent Negotiator: What to Say, What to Do, and How to Get What You Want—Every Time* (2002).

Charles Craver, *Effective Legal Negotiation and Settlement* (4th Ed. 2001).

John G. Cross, *The Economics of Bargaining* (1969).

Morton Deutsch & Peter T. Coleman, *The Handbook of Conflict Resolution: Theory & Practice* (2000).

John Patrick Dolan, *Negotiate Like the Pros* (1992).

Ted A. Donner & Brian L. Crowe, *Attorney's Practice Guide to Negotiations* (2d. Ed. 1995).

Daniel Druckman, *Negotiations: Social-psychological Perspectives* (1977).

Daniel Druckman et al., *Nonverbal Communication: Survey, Theory and Research* (1982).

Joel Edelman & Mary Beth Crain, *The Tao of Negotiation: How You Can Prevent, Resolve, and Transcend Conflict in Work and Everyday Life* (1993).

Julius Fast, *Body Language* (1970).

Roger Fisher & William Ury, *Getting to Yes: Negotiating Agreement Without Giving In* (Bruce Patton Ed., 2d Ed. 1991).

Xavier M. Frascogna, Jr. & H. Lee Hetherington, *The Lawyer's Guide to Negotiation: A Strategic Approach to Better Contracts and Settlements* (2001).

Xavier M. Frascogna, Jr. & H. Lee Hetherington, *Negotiation Strategy for Lawyers* (1984).

Donald G. Gifford, *Legal Negotiation: Theory and Applications* (1989).

Stephen B. Goldberg Et Al., *Dispute Resolution* (1985).

Alvin L. Goldman, *Settling for More: Mastering Negotiating Strategies and Techniques* (1991).

Francis Greenburger & Thomas Kiernan, *How to Ask for More and Get It: The Art of Creative Negotiation* (1978).

Julian Gresser, *Piloting Through Chaos: Wise Leadership, Effective Negotiation for the 21st Century* (1995).

P.h. Gulliver, Disputes And Negotiations: A Cross-cultural Perspective (1979).

Edward Twitchell Hall, *The Silent Language* (1959).

Judith A. Hall, *Nonverbal Sex Differences: Communication Accuracy and Expressive Style* (1984).

Ann Halpern, *Negotiating Skills* (1992).

Fen Osler Hampson & Michael Hart, *Multilateral Negotiations: Lessons from Arms Control, Trade, and the Environment* (1995).

Joseph D. Harbaugh, *Negotiation: Winning Tactics and Techniques* (1988).

Robert Gale Harper Et Al., *Nonverbal Communication: The State of the Art* (1978).

Dennis A. Hawver, *How to Improve Your Negotiation Skills* (1992).

Roger S. Haydock, *Negotiation Practice* (1984).

John M. Haynes & Gretchen L. Haynes, *Mediating Divorce: Casebook of Strategies for Successful Family Negotiations* (1989).

Robert D. Helsby Et Al., *The Evolving Process: Collective Negotiations in Public Employment* (1985).

Robert D. Helsby, *Portrait of a Process : Collective Negotiations in Public Employment / Public Employment Relations Services* (Muriel K. Gibbons Et Al. Eds., 1979).

Nancy Henley, *Body, Politics, Sex, and Nonverbal Communication* (1986).

Gregg M. Herman, *The Joy of Settlement: The Family Lawyer's Guide to Effective Negotiations and Settlement Strategies* (1997).

Jean M. Hiltrop & Shelia Udall, *The Essence of Negotiation* (1995).

Fred Charles Iklé., *How Nations Negotiate* (1964).

John Ilich, *Dealbreakers and Breakthroughs: The Ten Most Common and Costly Negotiation Mistakes and How to Overcome Them* (1992).

John Ilich.& Barbara Schindler Jones, *Successful Negotiation Skills for Women* (1981).

Norbert S. Jacker, *Effective Negotiation Techniques for Lawyers* (1984).

Fred Edmund Jandt, *Win Win Negotiating; Turning Conflict into Agreement* (1985).

Ralph A. Johnson, *Negotiation Basics: Concepts, Skills, and Exercises* (1993).

Chester Louis Karrass, *Give and Take: The Complete Guide to Negotiating Strategies and Tactics* (1993).

Chester Louis Karrass, *The Negotiating Game* (1970).

Karrass, G., *Negotiate to Close* (1985).

Gavin Kennedy, *The Perfect Negotiation* (1994).

Gavin Kennedy, *Pocket Negotiator* (1987).

Robert C. Knee & Robert C. Knee, Jr., *Collective Bargaining Clauses: Guideline Forms for Use in Labor Negotiations* (1975).

Deborah M. Kolb & Judith Williams, *Everyday Negotiation: Navigating the Hidden Agendas in Bargaining* (Rev. Ed. 2003).

Deborah M. Kolb & Judith Williams, *The Shadow Negotiation: How Women Can Master the Hidden Agendas That Determine Bargaining Success* (2000).

Korda, M., *Power! How to Get It, How to Use It* (1975).

Russell Korobkin, *Negotiation Theory and Strategy* (2002).

Stephen Kozicki, *Creative Negotiating: Proven Techniques for Getting What You Want From Any Negotiation* (1998).

Henry S. Kramer, *Game, Set, Match: Winning the Negotiations Game* (2001).

Roderick M. Kramer & David M. Messick, *Negotiation as a Social Process* (1995).

Victor A. Kremenyuk Et Al., *International Negotiation: Analysis, Approaches, Issues* (1991).

Phyllis Beck Kritek, *Negotiating at an Uneven Table: Developing Moral Courage in Resolving Our Conflicts* (2d Ed. 2002).

Robert Lawrence Kuhn, *Dealmaker: All the Negotiating Skills and Secrets You Need* (1988).

Amos Lakos, *International Negotiations: A Bibliography* (1989).

Arthur Samuel Lall, *Multilateral Negotiation and Mediation: Instruments and Methods* (1985).

Arthur Samuel Lall, *Modern International Negotiation* (1966).

David A. Lax, *The Manager as Negotiator: Bargaining for Cooperation and Competitive Gain* (1986).

Len Leritz, *No-fault Negotiating: A Simple and Innovative Approach for Solving Problems, Reaching Agreements, and Resolving Conflicts* (1990).

Paul Lesti Et Al., *Structured Settlements* (1986).

Rachelle L. Levitt & John J. Kirlin, *Managing Development Through Public / Private Negotiations* (1985).

Roy J. Lewicki Et Al., *Essentials of Negotiation* (3d Ed. 2004).

Roy J. Lewicki Et Al., *Negotiation: Readings, Exercises, and Cases* (4th Ed. 2003).

Roy J. Lewicki Et Al., *Think Before You Speak: The Complete Guide to Strategic Negotiation* (1996).

David V. Lewis, *Power Negotiation Tactics and Techniques* (1981).

Paul Michael Lisnek, *A Lawyer's Guide to Effective Negotiation and Mediation* (1993).

Grande Lum Et Al., *Expand the Pie: How to Add Value to Any Negotiation* (2003).

Frances Mautner-Markhof, *Processes of International Negotiations* (1989).

Bernard S. Mayer, *The Dynamics of Conflict Resolution: A Practitioner's Guide* (2000).

Brad Mcrae, *Negotiating and Influencing Skills: The Art of Creating and Claiming Value* (1998).

Albert Mehrabian, *Silent Messages: Implicit Communication of Emotions and Attitudes* (2d Ed. 1981).

Albert Mehrabian, *Nonverbal Communication* (1972).

Lee E. Miller & Jessica Miller, *A Woman's Guide to Successful Negotiating: How to Convince, Collaborate, and Create Your Way to Agreement* (2002).

George J. Mitchell, *Making Peace* (1999).

Robert H. Mnookin, *Beyond Winning: Negotiating to Create Value in Deals and Disputes* (2000).

Robert H. Mnookin Et Al., *Negotiating on Behalf of Others: Advice to Lawyers, Business Executives, Sports Agents, Diplomats, Politicians, and Everybody Else* (1999).

Ian E. Morley & Geoffrey M. Stephenson, *The Social Psychology of Bargaining* (1977).

Morrison, W., *The Prenegotiation Planning Book* (1985).

William F. Morrison & Henry H. Calero, *The Human Side of Negotiations* (1994).

J. Keith Murnighan, *Bargaining Games: A New Approach to Strategic Thinking in Negotiations* (1992).

J. Keith Murnighan, *The Dynamics Of Bargaining Games* (1991).

Margaret A. Neale & Max H. Bazerman, *Cognition and Rationality in Negotiation* (1991).

Richard G. Neal, *Negotiations Strategies: A Reference Manual for Public Sector Labor Negotiations* (1981).

Richard G. Neal, *Bargaining Tactics: A Reference Manual for Public Sector Labor Negotiations* (1980).

Richard G. Neal, *Retrieval Bargaining: A Guide for Public Sector Labor Negotiations* (1981).

Wade J. Newhouse, *Public Sector Labor Relations Law in New York State: The Law Relating to Public Employee Organization, Negotiations, Resolution of Disputes, and Enforcement Of Agreements* (1978).

Richard P. Nielsen, *The Politics of Ethics: Methods for Acting, Learning, and Sometimes Fighting with Others in Addressing Ethics Problems in Organizational Life* (1996).

Gerard I. Nierenberg, *The Complete Negotiator* (1991).

Gerard I. Nierenberg, *The Art of Negotiating* (1987).

Gerard I. Nierenberg, *Fundamentals of Negotiating* (1973).

Gerard I. Nierenberg & Henry H. Calero, *How to Read a Person Like a Book* (1971).

Juliet Nierenberg & Irene S. Ross, *Negotiate for Success: Effective Strategies for Realizing Your Goals* (2003).

Louise Nieuwmeijer, *Negotiation: Methodology and Training* (1992).

Personal Injury Valuation Handbooks (Jury Verdict Research, Inc.).

Stephen M. Pollan & Mark Levine, *The Total Negotiator* (1994).

Peter J. Poulopoulos, *Negotiating Tips: A Practical Guide to Be a Successful Negotiator and Obtain Results* (1996).

Program on Negotiation at Harvard Law School, *Negotiation: Strategies for Mutual Gain* (Lavinia Hall Ed., 1993).

Dean G. Pruitt, *Negotiation Behavior* (1981).

DEAn G. Pruitt & Peter J. Carnevale, *Negotiation in Social Conflict* (1993).

Howard Raiffa, *The Art and Science of Negotiation* (1982).

Howard Raiffa Et Al., *Negotiation Analysis: The Science and Art of Collaborative Decision Making* (2002).

Bernard A. Ramundo, *Effective Negotiation: A Guide to Dialogue Management and Control* (1992).

Bernard A. Ramundo, *Effective Negotiation: A Primer* (1984).

L.n. Rangarajan, *The Limitation of Conflict: A Theory of Bargaining and Negotiation* (1985).

Ross R. Reck & Brian G. Long, *The Win-win Negotiator* (1985).

Linda Richardson, *Winning Negotiation Strategies for Bankers* (1987).

Robert J. Ringer, *Winning Through Intimidation* (1974).

Jeffrey Z. Rubin & Bert R. Brown, *The Social Psychology of Bargaining and Negotiation* (1975).

Raymond Saner, *The Expert Negotiator: Strategy, Tactics, Motivation, Behaviour, Leadership* (2000).

Nicholas Reid Schaffzin, *Negotiate Smart* (1997).

Nicholas Reid Schaffzin, *Don't Be a Chump!: Negotiating Skills You Need* (1995).

Michael Schatzki & Wayne R. Coffey, *Negotiation: The Art of Getting What You Want* (1981).

Mark K. Schoenfield & Rick M. Schoenfield, *Legal Negotiations: Getting Maximum Results* (1988).

G. Richard Shell, *Bargaining for Advantage: Negotiation Strategies for Reasonable People* (1999).

Sidney Siegel & Lawrence E. Fouraker, *Bargaining and Group Decision Making: Experiments in Bilateral Monopoly* (1977).

James R. Silkenat & Jeffrey M. Aresty, *A Guide to International Business Negotiations: A Comparison of Cross-cultural Issues and Successful Approaches* (2d Ed. 2000).

Michael Spangle & Myra Warren Isenhart, *Negotiation: Communication for Diverse Settings* (2003).

Donald B. Sparks, *The Dynamics of Effective Negotiation* (1982).

Philip Sperber, *Attorney's Practice Guide to Negotiations* (1985).

Mike R. Stark, *The Power of Negotiating: Strategies for Success* (1996).

Anslem L. Strauss, *Negotiations: Varieties, Contexts, Processes, and Social Order* (1978).

Larry L. Teply, *Legal Negotiation in a Nutshell* (1992).

O.C. Tirella & Gary D. Bates, *Win-win Negotiating: A Professional's Playbook* (1993).

Trial Lawyers Section and the Committee on Continuing Legal Education of the New York State Bar Association, *Secrets of Successful Evaluation Negotiation and Settlement Techniques in Civil Cases* (1985).

William Ury, *Getting Past No: Negotiation Your Way from Confrontation to Cooperation* (1993).

William Ury, *Getting Past No: Negotiating with Difficult People* (1991).

Roger J. Volkema, *The Negotiation Toolkit: How to Get Exactly What You Want in Any Business or Personal Situation* (1999).

John Von Neumann & Oskar Morgenstern, *Theory of Games and Economic Behavior* (1944).

James A. Wall, Jr., *Negotiation, Theory and Practice* (1985).

Michael A. Walker & George L. Harris, *Negotiations: Six Steps to Success* (1995).

Tessa Albert Warschaw, *Winning by Negotiation* (1980).

Robert A. Wenke, *The Art of Negotiation for Lawyers* (1985).

Gerald R. Williams, *Legal Negotiation and Settlement* (1983).

Gerald R. Williams, *A Lawyer's Handbook for Effective Negotiation and Settlement* (1981).

Gerald R. Williams, *Handbook on Effectiveness in Legal Negotiation: A System for Maximizing Negotiator Effectiveness* (1977).

Donald H. Wollet & Robert H. Channin, *The Law and Practice of Teacher Negotiations* (1974).

Oran R. Young, *Bargaining: Formal Theories of Negotiation* (1975).

I. William Zartman, *The Negotiation Process: Theories and Applications* (1978).

I. William Zartman & Maureen R. Berman, *The Practical Negotiator* (1982).

Index

Arbitration, Mediation, and Negotation Books from NITA

Alternatives to Litigation: Mediation, Arbitration, and the Art of Dispute Resolution
by Abraham P. Ordover and Andrea Doneff
2d ed., 270 pp., © 2002, ISBN 1-55681-749-5

Arbitration Advocacy
by John W. Cooley with Steven Lubet
2d ed., 598 pp., © 2003, ISBN 1-55681-799-1

The Arbitrator's Handbook
by John W. Cooley
2d ed, 469 pp., © 2005, ISBN 1-55681-916-1

The Art of Mediation
by Mark Bennett and Scott Hughes
2d ed, © 2005, ISBN 1-55681-865-3

Mediation Advocacy
by John W. Cooley
2d ed, 472 pp., © 2002, ISBN 1-55681-780-0

Mediation Representation: Advocating in a Problem-Solving Process
by Harold I. Abramson
470 pp, © 2004, ISBN 1-55681-821-1

The Mediator's Handbook
by John W. Cooley
450 pp., © 2002, ISBN 1-55681-681-2

To order go to
the Web site at www.nita.org
or call (800) 225-6482